# Acclaim for *Got An Angry Kid?*
# and The P.A.C.T. Training Program

"Dr. Gibson, a renowned Parent Educator has spent years refining his techniques for treating "Bad Boys." Those who have followed Dr. Gibson's edicts have seen their bad children returned to them as functional pleasant human beings. I urge all parents, especially those with difficult children, to read Dr. Gibson's book and follow the wise advice you find therein."

> Richard H. Bloomer Ed.E. ABPS, FACAPP, FACFE
> Emeritus Professor, The University of Connecticut,
> Certified Neuropsychologist,
> M.S. Clinical Psychopharmacology

"Although I was only a few weeks into P.A.C.T., I felt myself becoming calmer, more hopeful and more in control. P.A.C.T. Is putting life into my parenting. P.A.C.T. does what three years of residential placement didn't."

> Mrs. K.C., Middletown, CT, single Mom of a seriously emotionally disturbed boy

"I thank God every day for being enrolled in P.A.C.T."

> Ms. R.R., Middletown, CT, single Mom of an out-of-control daughter

"When Dr. Gibson first came to my home, I was angry. My son was angrier. My household was total chaos. My husband and son were always yelling at each other. My son was in total control. This is not so anymore. P.A.C.T. has stopped the anger."

> Mrs. D.R., Putnam, CT, Mom in a blended family

"If P.A.C.T. were used more often it could prevent many kids from having to be taken from their homes. It is a GREAT tool. My only regret is that we didn't get involved with P.A.C.T. sooner. Our daughter has changed considerably."

> Mr. & Mrs. R.S., Andover, CT, Parents of an out-of-control daughter

"I was hesitant to start P.A.C.T. Now I can effectively communicate without displaying anger. I now listen. My relationship with my son has greatly improved."

> Mrs. E.D., Danbury, CT, single Mom of an out-of-control son

"We are grateful for P.A.C.T. It seemed too simple at first. How wrong we were! As weeks passed we changed as our children changed and life became livable again. Compared to what our life was before P.A.C.T., everyday is a bed of roses. P.A.C.T. Gave us a second chance."

> Mr. & Mrs. R.B., Woodstock, CT, Parents of a severely disturbed daughter

# Got An Angry Kid?

We have a solution.

Parenting Spike:
A Difficult Child

^
Seriously

## by Andrew D. Gibson, Ph.D.

Library of Congress Cataloging-in-Publication Data

Gibson, Andrew D., 1945-
Got an angry kid? parenting Spike: a seriously difficult child / by Andrew D. Gibson.
    p. cm.
  Includes bibliographical references and index.
  ISBN-13: 978-1-932690-89-7 (trade paper : alk. paper)
  ISBN-10: 1-932690-89-1 (trade paper : alk. paper)
  1. Anger in children. 2. Anger in adolescence. 3. Attitude change in children. 4. Parenting. 5. Child rearing.
  6. Problem children—Behavior modification. I. Title.
  BF723.A4G53 2009
  649'.154--dc22        2009009517

"Parenting Angry Children and Teens," "P.A.C.T.," "Parenting the Unparentable Child," and "Got An Angry Kid?" are service marks of Intensive Behavior Management Training, LLC. No individual or agency may claim to offer Parenting Angry Children and Teens who has not been P.A.C.T.-certified by Intensive Behavior Management Training LLC. Inquiries about finding participating individuals or agencies, or inquires into certification requirements should be directed to:

Andrew D. Gibson, Ph.D.
Intensive Behavior Management Training LLC
P.O. Box 238
Windham, Connecticut 06280-0238

Email: Agibson@snet.net
www.DrAGibson.com

Published by
Loving Healing Press
5145 Pontiac Trail
Ann Arbor, Michigan 48105-9627
Tollfree: 888-761-6268
Fax: 734-663-6861
Email: info@LHPress.com

*Redefining what is possible for healing mind and spirit since 2003.*

# Acknowledgements

This book couldn't have seen the light of day without the following friends who read one or more of the many drafts. Their contributions, wisdom, and support were invaluable:

Bruce Clements, Virginia Fulton, Deborah Walsh, Gail Karlitz, Renee Esordi, Shirley Mustard, and Stefan Szafarek.

In an effort to respect confidentiality and privacy, all discussions of former cases in *Got An Angry Kid?* are compilations. Spike is a fictionalized treatment of a real child.

"My Name is Spike and I pretty much hate you."

# Table of Contents

Parenting Spike is the 28-step P.A.C.T. parent survival program. Readers are given a roadmap for managing their difficult family. The steps in parenting Spike are presented in two chapters:

Spike is on poor terms with the school principal.

# Preface

## The Author's Biography

I was born one soft spring day in 1945 in Detroit toward the end of World War II. I was the third of four children. My Dad once told me that he sired his children in an effort to keep himself out of the draft. It didn't work. He was called up, made it as far as boot camp but was sent home: VJ Day arrived. So, three toddlers later, he and my mother had clearly developed a fondness for each other. It lasted for 65 years. Other than that, all he had to show for his time spent avoiding the military was an army blanket. He wasn't even in long enough to qualify for a veteran's-preferred job. But we survived. There are worse ways to start life. There are also better ones. I grew up in a small farming town in Michigan. We didn't farm. Dad was the biology teacher at the local high school. He wasn't much cut out for that and finally made the transition to community college teaching—a position he held until his retirement.

I remember most of my elementary school teachers and can name them in sequence to this day. Mrs. Osgood was my kindergarten teacher. She loved me. My fourth-grade teacher was Miss Duffer. She didn't love me. What a beast that woman was. But I learned my multiplication tables as well as learned to have disabling headaches which continued for many years. Once past the third grade, my teachers found me less and less charming. There was something about my need to be charming, coupled with a world that demands more than charm, which prompted a vast range of misfitting tendencies. Life was slowly turning brutal. The headaches were just the canary in the mineshaft. It was about this time that I swallowed a bunch of aspirin. I really don't think I wanted to kill myself. I knew I was very interested in getting close. I wanted someone to stop the misery, yet nothing happened. On the bright side, I didn't have a headache that day. On the less bright side, I was still me. I will leave the meaning of this up to those better prepared to understand it. Anyway, I didn't try it again.

My parents were, in the face of this, like deer caught in the headlights—surprised, disbelieving, and unprepared. Of course they cared, but they didn't know what to do because they lacked the courage to understand. Love was never an issue, but just because they loved each other doesn't mean that they could effectively parent their kids, all of whom still hobble about to one degree or another. So they took me to a shrink. ME!! What about them? It was, in short, a childhood that didn't leave me ready to be an adult, much less a parent. I couldn't avoid the former, but I probably shouldn't have been the latter. However, that doesn't stop most of us, and it didn't stop me. It didn't stop my Dad either, may he rest in peace. He, after all, got in to the parent business to avoid the Army.

Everything about my childhood and my experience as a parent went into what became P.A.C.T. Training and the book, *Got An Angry Kid?* One of the really great things about life is that you get second chances. Not that you get to replay the same tapes over again. You can't. Once something has happened, it has happened. But you can figure out what went wrong and work like hell to make it better. Your childhood is foisted upon you. Your adulthood is yours to make. YOU are the key here. Not THEM, be they your parents or your kids. We get one set of each and have to learn what makes them special. Along the way, we have to stop complaining and stop waiting for everyone to change so we'll be happy. The best defense is a good offense. Learn to create it yourself. P.A.C.T. is all about taking ourselves by the ear, trotting us in front of the bathroom mirror and saying, "Look at yourself!" The program and the book are my opportunities to exculpate myself and pass onto other parents a lot of what I have learned.

On the way to adulthood, I got my BA and MA from San Diego State University. I elected to stay in San Diego after discharge from the Navy during the Vietnam War. I then taught briefly at Portland State University in Oregon and the University of Maine, Presque Isle, before completing the Ph.D. at the University of Connecticut in 1987. I had the marvelously brilliant Richard Bloomer for an advisor. We remain friends to this day. I couldn't have developed P.A.C.T. without him even though he had nothing to do with the actual program design. It is his approach to learning that spurred P.A.C.T.'s development.

I put the bones of the program together just as one of my sons was turning into Spike before my eyes. Spike, as you will see, is the antihero of *Got An Angry Kid?* I didn't know what to do with my own Spike. I just acted on a hunch. But it was a hunch that proved correct—quit trying to be the parent you obviously can't be. Everything else was flesh hung on the bones of this idea. It took me three years to achieve, in my own family, something that now takes me less than a year to teach to others. I had only the occasional client to work with until the Connecticut State Department of Children and Families stepped forward and asked me to create an official program in 1993. Since then, some 500 families have gone through the program. The success rate has always been high, and it has been a gratifying experience to tell families, "I know what you are going through, but there are lights at the end of the tunnel if you are willing to make some substantial changes in how you approach your kid."

I was asked recently if I was a Spike. I said, "No, that's somebody else." I was the kid who would have happily taken a shotgun to school but that was way before blowing away classmates became a common way of demonstrating unhappiness. My Dad also didn't own one, which probably helped. Thankfully for me, and hopefully for you, I lived to share the tale.

I now live in northeastern Connecticut with my wife of 40 years and enjoy good relationships with my sons, both of whom seem to have turned out fine. I enjoy a wide circle of friends. Yet, I'm still occasionally beset with the feelings of being the lonely kid that dominated my childhood, that sent me in a direction I didn't want to go, and made re-routing myself so challenging. My story doesn't have to be your story to make the program work for you. We acquire the Spikes in our lives many different ways. This story is only one of them.

Dr. Andrew Gibson

Anaïs Nin said, "The only abnormality is the incapacity to love."

P.A.C.T. says, this is fortunate because as out of whack as Spike seems, he still has the potential to accept and give love. You'll see.

# PART I
## Understanding Spike

Spike doesn't like shrinks and resents it when he is dragged into one of their offices.

# CHAPTER 1 : Introduction to P.A.C.T. (Parenting Angry Children and Teens)

*Got An Angry Kid* features a self-help program called, Parenting Angry Children and Teens (P.A.C.T.). It is directed to parents of out-of-control children. Those children are seemingly unparentable.

- **Out-of-control means what it says—parents no longer control their child.** Unparentable means what it says, too. There is little the parent can do in the name of reward or punishment that works.
- *Got An Angry Kid?* **introduces Spike and his family.** Spike and his family tell the P.A.C.T. story. His family is defined by his out-of-control behavior. Spike may resemble your child. Spike didn't become Spike as a result of some cataclysmic event. He could have. He just didn't. As it happens, his story is benign compared to many. It doesn't really matter. There are lots of ways of making children miserable. Most of them are benign and unintentional.
- **Spike is both worldly and naive.** He is, after all, a child. Don't expect him to understand a lot of what goes on around him. He does and he doesn't. He needs his parents to fill in the gaps, but he won't accept them.
- **Spike is miserable.** He needs treatment for emotional disturbance, but he won't accept it, either. He is miserable both to himself and to those around him.
- **The goal of the book is to get Spike's family to function as a family Spike's parents must change how they interact with their son.** *Got An Angry Kid?* will show parents how to restore control. Spike's misery will seem much less significant.

> Spike's parents need to recoup lost respect. But Spike will never give it if he can't learn to value his parents first. Parental attempts to get his respect by asserting themselves on him will keep him fighting. Forget telling him what to do. It's a losing strategy. Instead, back off.

If the answer to *Got An Angry Kid?* is, "Yes," then a piece of cold comfort is that you have lots of company. The woods are full of Spikes. Many of them are friends of your child. But, you probably knew that already.

- **None of their parents like your child any more than you like theirs.** The fact that your child acts awful and hangs around others just like him is a problem. It will take something special to get his attention. That something special is you.
- **The parent who can answer the question,** *Got An Angry Kid?* **with a "Yes" is miles ahead of the parent who is still asking, "If only I knew what was troubling my child."** Getting to "Yes" is a milestone many parents can't achieve. If the answer is "Yes," then the next question is, "Angry at whom?" Like it or not, deserve it or not, your child is focusing his anger onto YOU.
- **Spike's behavior is a risky inconvenience.** Problems magnify if they linger into adulthood. He will take his emotional baggage and produce failed marriages, failed jobs and failed children. He will blame you. He will also swear he will do a better job of parenting. It isn't true. He hasn't the foundation. There is nothing on the horizon to suggest that he will get it.
- **Parents teach P.A.C.T.'s 28 goals to themselves.** The process takes about a year. You will have a calmer, more respectful and optimistic family. The difference is often dramatic.
- **How rotten does Spike have to be?** There is no law that says you have to have a child as awful as Spike before you learn P.A.C.T. However, most parents wait until their child is Spike-like, which is too bad. It is not too late, but it sure isn't any easier.

> Practice P.A.C.T. on your whole family, on the whole town. Don't just concentrate on Spike. Spike will calm down and his sister, the easy one, will pick up where he left off. It's temporary, but it will happen. You need to be prepared.

- **P.A.C.T. is not clinical.** P.A.C.T. doesn't figure out why the child is angry. That is a question for therapy. We accept that he is angry. The child controls the atmosphere of the household. No one is spared. He gets anger in return for his behavior. He seems to thrive on it. That must stop. For his sake and for your sake.
- **P.A.C.T. can change the parent vs. child struggle in your home.** Changes occur because parents care enough to adjust how they parent their Spike.
- **P.A.C.T. concentrates on getting rid of parenting that's going nowhere fast.** Behavior that works will gradually emerge both in the parent and then in the child. The parent takes the lead.
- **There is a lagtime of approximately eight weeks between parent change and child change.** P.A.C.T. challenges every assumption you have about parenting. Most assumptions will be replaced. The child will wait to see how serious you are before adjusting himself.
- **P.A.C.T. works best in conflict.** Conflict drives parents to participate. Conflict ebbs as the parent learns. It will become clear that the child's behavior and the parent's learning are linked.

What do parents learn?

- That they are in a codependent relationship with a child.
- That they have become victims.
- That victims act in stereotyped and counterproductive ways.
- That everything traditionally passing for parenting can enable the behavior parents say they don't want.
- That boundaries between parent and child have broken down.
- That the parental ineffectiveness and childhood opposition feed on one another, creating codependence.
- That the need to fix the child needs to be augmented by fixing the parenting style.

Cake mixes have directions. So does P.A.C.T. They are:

- **Learn one goal at a time.**
- **Do not go to the next goal if you have more than four errors.**
- **Whenever your error rate goes above four errors, stop.**
- **Repeat the weakest goal until the error rate declines to four or fewer.** Simple.

**If you think this is tough, consider the prospect of living with your child for the rest of your life.** The more insecure children are, the closer they stay to home. They rightly suspect that you will always bail them out, emotionally and otherwise. They will cycle between needing you and rejecting you. You don't want that. You want them to stabilize.

In P.A.C.T., you will redefine how you parent Spike. You will lose spontaneity, but you also lose every unworkable parenting impulse you ever had. Given the peace you get, it isn't a bad trade. If you anticipate, then you are prepared. If you are in control only of yourself, that's plenty. If you can't direct, then you support. If you wait to be asked, you'll be asked. The willingness to act in a supporting role becomes the gift of patience.

# Don't Look Now...

Here is what you learn if you want to de-Spike your home. Between the two of them, Spike's parents commit most of the following errors every day. Most days their tactics backfire, allowing Spike to think he is still in control. P.A.C.T. took these errors in parenting the out-of-control child and turned them into goals. Do some of them feel familiar? They should. You probably violate them, too. They are the keys to taming Spike. If you want Spike's cooperation, you must practice eliminating these on everyone. If you focus on Spike, the practicing won't work. Your task is not merely changing your interaction with Spike. You must change your interactions everywhere so that you don't run the danger of bringing them back to Spike.

1. No yelling
2. No showing anger
3. No failure to distract yourself so your annoyance doesn't turn into yelling or anger
4. No getting caught by surprise and over-reacting
5. No threatening
6. No swearing
7. No lousy tone of voice
8. No sarcasm
9. No criticism or fault-finding
10. No nagging, reminding, or repeating
11. No forgetting to follow through
12. No preaching, lecturing or giving unwanted and unsolicited advice
13. No deals
14. No allowing your buttons to be pushed
15. No demanding
16. No accusing
17. No arguing
18. No complaining
19. No namecalling
20. No talking so damn much
21. No questioning
22. No frustration
23. No initiating conversation
24. No dredging up the past
25. No explaining or justifying yourself
26. No negativity
27. No passive-aggressive nonsense
28. No waffling or inconsistency

# P.A.C.T.'s experience suggests you have one of two reactions to the list:

1. "This looks so simple any idiot could do it!"
or
2. "Oh, my God, you expect me to learn all that?"

If you have reaction number one, you don't have a problem. You clearly don't have a Spike. You may not even have any kids at all. What's worse, you probably don't understand parents who are in this pickle or face the challenge of reversing every parental impulse they have. This means you will have a hard time supporting a parent who identifies with the goals. Unfortunately, those parents who have reaction number two know that you don't understand them, don't sympathize with them and don't have patience for them. They feel isolated as a result.

If you have reaction number two, you are bowled over, don't know where to begin, and you think this is impossible. That means you are connecting with the list. And that makes you a prime candidate for reading further.

So, peel yourself off the floor and let's think about this. Yes, the list looks overwhelming but many parents have gotten through it so don't worry: You will, too. Is it hard? Sure, it's hard, quite possibly the hardest thing you will ever do. It is like losing 100 pounds. What makes it hard? You will be required to change how you parent. Period. These are not 28 suggestions; they are 28 requirements. Unlike diets, however, once you learn P.A.C.T., you probably won't slip back into failure. You will be changed forever.

You can learn P.A.C.T. if you like your Spike a little. If you despise him, you won't get far. This program requires self-discipline in the name of love. It may seem like a gift your Spike doesn't deserve. If that is what you think, you have a shoe on the wrong foot: Stop concentrating on Spike. Concentrate on yourself. If you take care of you, then Spike will take care of himself. For better or worse—and admit it, it's been mostly for worse—you have been concentrating on Spike for a long time. Spike has become the family centerpiece. It's time to get some flowers instead.

At this point, you can turn to Part II, which is the program, and get to work. Or, you can keep on reading the Introduction. Or, you can flip back and forth. Do whatever works for you.

And, by the way, the list isn't a random collection. The list represents a universal set of enabling behaviors parents use hoping their child will change. He won't. These enable the behavior you say you don't want. You can keep these and self-righteously defend your right to be angry. If so, you will feed your kid's insatiable need to oppose you. Or, you can give them all up, thereby removing the single most important source of disapproval, rejection, and criticism your child has in his life: YOU. If you do the latter, you will be rewarded. If you continue the former, you will set your kid up for failure.

We assume since you've read this far that you are willing to consider giving up the former. Wonderful. Now, back to work....

Spike doesn't much like his family, his sister most of all.

# CHAPTER 2 : Meet Spike and His Family

## A Portrait of a Dysfunctional American Family

**Spike is angry, surly, and mean.**

His behavior tells us that he feels someone has driven over him with a tank. He feels confused, scared, alone, and stupid. He doesn't often use those terms, at least not directly. He acts them out. He fights without a moment's notice. Everything becomes a target, and his parents are the handiest. Fighting is easier than thinking. Thinking feels bad and makes him depressed.

Spike lives with his parents and an idiot sister. His Mom is always saying, "Spike, honey, you shouldn't talk to your mother that way." Sometimes his Mom cries when he talks bad to her. Sometimes she screams at him. "For what? 'Cause I called you a bitch? Big deal," Spike snips.

And his Dad? "That loser?" Spike snorts, "He gets all puffed up and says, 'Spike, I'm warning you!'"

"You should see it. Dad looks ridiculous, all serious and worked up. I laugh myself sick sometimes. His warnings are nothing. I suppose he thinks he can make me sit in a corner. Forget it! I'm not sitting in any fucking corner for him or anyone else. He can kiss my ass."

Spike's disrespect is a clue that his future is in doubt. He will look for rebellion. He may cover his body in tattoos and shout that he is unique. He will insist he needs no one as no one measures up to his uniqueness. He will edge away from the mainstream. He will push away those who might like to know him. He will profess his uniqueness too loudly. Actually, he will fear the rejection he is likely to get.

Yet his choices, without a change in attitude, have disappeared. He won't need to worry about a future. It's been decided for him. He can start practicing this useful career mantra right now:

"You want fries with that, mister?"

**The Rest of the Family**

We have Mom, Dad, the annoyingly perfect Angelique and, of course, Spike with his faithful bulldog, Ruff. You can see that Spike is about to push Angelique into the next county. We don't know what Angelique did. Maybe she whispered, "'Tard!" in his ear. If so, she may as well have lit his hair on fire. If she did whisper in his ear, she whispered quietly, so her folks wouldn't hear. She did it so that she could get a reaction from Spike; so she could scream, "Mommy! Mommy! Do something!"

Both Mommy and Daddy pick up their cues: "Spike, you are such a bully! What's the matter with you? How'd you like a taste of your own medicine?"

And then they comfort poor Angelique: "We're so sorry, sweetheart. Would ice cream make you feel better? Come sit on my lap."

All that parental honey makes risking a sock in the head worthwhile. Every whimper makes Spike despise her more. Spike, after all, has a lousy reputation. If something is wrong, Spike is assumed to be in the middle. That's because he generally is. But Mom and Dad learn too slowly that Angelique isn't always as innocent as she pretends.

> Nothing they do makes a difference— not therapy, not drugs, not special programs, not in-home services.

Mom and Dad are a professional couple. They married early. They had their children later, stitching together an education and career. Family wasn't always first priority. Spike, the first born, was pressured as first-born boys sometimes are. These folks had their limitations as young parents do. They both came from families that had problems, although they are certain they are superior to those old family problems. But, their hands are now full. They've watched Spike get worse. Nothing they do makes a difference—not therapy, not drugs, not special programs, not in-home services. For one thing, those services are often given by twenty-something human service workers who are cheap hires for their agencies but who have no clue what it's like to live with a child like Spike. There is nothing wrong with them that time and the right experience won't cure, assuming they can put up with the low pay and occasional brutal experiences to get it.

Even when Spike's folks encounter a professional their age, a gulf of inexperience remains. His folks feel guilty when they can't make everyone's advice work, and they also resent the advice. After all, they really don't know what to do, so they try everything. Everyone, they say, brims with authority about how to proceed although nobody has actually lived the program they promote. This becomes a problem.

Spike's folks lose confidence. All those appointments are like Al-Anon meetings without a recovering drunk for a leader. Everyone bases their experience with normal children. Spike isn't normal. None of the programs make many demands on Spike's folks, other than to insist they "put boundaries around that child" or give assurance that they will drive Spike from one appointment to another. P.A.C.T.'s idea that the mess be dumped on parental shoulders seems preposterous. They tried family counseling thinking that if they talked out their problems, everything would be better. Spike disagreed. Getting him to the appointment wasn't worth the hell he made it. He hated being there. First, he said he wasn't crazy, they were. Second, it wasn't a simple matter of telling his folks how he felt, not that he knew how he felt anyway. He was confused about how he felt. He was sure they'd never understand. All he wanted was to be left alone, providing, of course, he could be in charge. He has no desire to negotiate away his right to be angry.

Spike's Dad is a good guy, but he's wrapped up in his own world. He's too preoccupied to engage his family. He is a hard worker, creative, has scads of friends, a non-stop social life but lives in the future. He is independent to a fault and refuses to be pushed. It all comes at a price. Spike feels his Dad is never 'there.' Life with Spike's Mom is a struggle. His folks love each other, but they don't complement one another; they compete. Spike sees the struggle, but doesn't see the love. Spike's Dad is an illustration of how love without engagement feels like rejection to a little child.

Spike's Mom is a highly involved Mom, but she is also a controller, demanding, loud, insistent and always right. She doesn't show respect easily although she insists on it for herself. She can be unkind but expects kindness in return. She won't accept blame and can't stand to be poked at in fun. She is a professional woman who is hard working, bright and thoroughly dedicated to her family. She is a traditional Mom in the cookie baking tradition. She can be loving and giving, but her love comes at a price. She gives orders. She reminds everyone about everything and always nags. She is a committed back seat driver. She is an illustration of how love without tolerance feels like rejection to a little child.

> It all comes at a price. Spike feels his Dad is never 'there.' Life with Spike's Mom is a struggle. His folks love each other, but they don't complement one another; they compete. Spike sees the struggle, but doesn't see the love.

So, we have a child who needs therapy but won't accept it. We have parents who are searching for a solution they can believe in but can't find. Desperation worms its way in.

Spike's sister, Angelique is insufferable. First, "the little shit," as Spike calls her, is nearly perfect. Second, she makes sure Spike knows it. They pretty much hate each other. Spike has no problem punching her if she steps across the line. He gets a roar of parent anger whenever he hits her, but he doesn't care. She irritates him on purpose. He unfailingly obliges a reaction. She then runs screaming as if the world is coming to an end. But she returns to do it again. She gets preferential treatment from her parents. They always speak nicely to her. Spike, on the other hand, must suffer their sarcasm, their nasty tone of voice and their assumption that he is always wrong. She is good if for no other reason than Spike is bad. But Spike wouldn't follow her lead if his life depended on it. It is a matter of pride for both. If he is to be convicted before he opens his mouth, so be it.

She, on the other hand, wins the spelling bee, has acceptable friends and doesn't generate irate phone calls from the school. Spike gets himself thrown off the bus, not Angelique. "Why can't you be more like your sister?" the school says, which just sets his teeth on edge.

But Angelique has her resentments. She gets tired of being good since it doesn't get her a whole lot. She has to live with this "tard" of a brother. The atmosphere in the house is often poisonous. She can't bring her friends around because he is likely to antagonize them. She can't figure out why her folks allow this to go on and on. If it were up to her, she'd pound him until he quit being a brat.

Angelique says, "Why do you let him get away with that?"

Parents reply, "What do you want us to do, beat him?"

Angelique retorts, "Get rid of him, that's what I want. Make him live some other place. I can't stand it here. MAKE HIM STOP!"

Angelique blames her parents, her father most of all, for the awful home and for that jerk of a brother who lives in it.

## Spike's Dog Ruff

Every boy needs a dog. But Ruff is more than a dog. Ruff is a statement. By the looks of Spike, you might not guess he needs protection from anything. But, you'd be wrong. Spike tries to control everything by keeping everything away. Ruff is his advance guard. You want Spike? Deal first with Ruff. Most folks don't deal, which makes Spike feel lousy.

Sound backwards? Probably, but not much about his life is straightforward. You see, Spike hasn't a clue why he feels the way he feels, and the best he can do is put up this huge front and dare you to do something about it. Both he and Ruff are ready for a fight. The longer he relies on the front, which includes Ruff, to get him through the day, the longer it will take him to get rid of it. He actually doesn't like the front, but it's better than nothing, and nothing is pretty much what he expects from his parents. He is waiting for his parents to get smart, but doubts they will.

If Spike's parents wait until he is 25 to get smart (in other words, to change how they interact with him) there will be a lot of bad experience stuck to the bottom of his shoe. They will also be grandparents of teenagers. What they don't know is that both Spike and Ruff are open to change, but neither of them trust. They want you to walk over hot coals to reach them. But they still want you to reach them. Words mean nothing. They've heard them all. Honeyed words are sooner or later followed by foul words in the form of nagging, whining, complaining, threatening, etc. So don't even bother. Think you can reward him with doggy treats and he will love you forever? Ruff will snatch the bones from your hands, stuff his face, and then bite you. As far as Ruff is concerned, he is entitled to every treat you can produce and then some. Rewards don't work. Punishment? You're kidding, right? You think you can punish Ruff? If you chain him to his dog house one day, do you really think he will fetch your slippers, paper, and pipe the next? Ruff is a four-pawed metaphor for Spike. Ruff and Spike look at the world similarly.

> He actually doesn't like the front, but it's better than nothing, and nothing is pretty much what he expects from his parents. He is waiting for his parents to get smart, but doubts they will.

Neither Ruff nor Spike have confidence in Spike's parents. They misinterpret every kindness. They assume threat. They expect the worst. Now what? Forget about Spike and Ruff. Concentrate on yourself.

Spike's dog Ruff. More than a dog, Ruff is a statement.

Spike and his scruffy friends.

Got An Angry Kid?

# CHAPTER 3 : Spike's Story

## Spike Tells Us What it's Like to Be Abnormal

The following is a series of five interviews conducted with Spike by a professor at the local college. He wanted to interview Spike to get his opinions on what it is like to be an unhappy child for a book he was writing. Spike agreed but only because the guy promised to pay him. Spike doesn't do anything for free. The remarks have been edited for brevity and readability

"They think I'm terrible. 'Course, they're right. I am. They haven't a clue why, though. Probably never will. I do anything I please, whenever I want. They're just a bunch of phonies. They say they care, but if I wait 30 seconds, they are back to the same old thing. They yell a lot. Everything I do is wrong. Then there is all the blame. And nag, nag, nag. I need them to go away…just leave me alone.

"I know how to be good. It isn't a mystery. I haven't been good for a while, but I could get back into it if I wanted. But I don't really want to. They don't like the kids I hang with, that's why I hang with them, just to piss them off. It works too. These other kids aren't so bad. Not really. Well, some of them are. They come from worse places than I do. They hate their parents, too. Mostly for good reason.

Spike has friends: Little Fred, Stella, Sugar, Jesus, Leroy, Zeke to name a few. Everyone has friends because everybody needs somebody. The difference between this set of friends and everyone else's is these are all misfits. They all have struggles they deal with poorly. Spike's friends are hardly welcome at his parent's home. What little his parents know of these friends, they don't like. But, other parents feel the same way about Spike. All the parents are right—these kids are a bad influence on one another. These friends tend to hold one another down. They don't get together in the evening as a study group. What they do in the evening is often immoral, illegal, or both. Spike won't make much progress as long as he hangs out with them, but normal friends don't want him. Spike's parents have no control over this or anything else. What to do? Spike must give these friends up if he is to be successful. The good news is that he probably will. The bad news is that it'll take a while. The difference lies with his parents. Even though they swear they have no influence, they actually do.

"Anyway, we do what we want 'cause nobody can make us do different. The more they try, the more we laugh in their face. Why not? So where were my folks when I needed them? Who knows. Sure weren't in my corner. Parents come first all the time. Know how many times we've moved in the last five years? Six times. You know what it is like to move, make a friend, move again? It sucks. You never know where you are going to wake up."

"My parents don't get along. Mom is always pissed at my Dad."

"Why don't you do something?" she yells.

"Just what exactly did you have in mind?" he yells back.

"Anything. I don't care. If you just weren't so selfish," she says.

"She yells about money, too. Dad swears back. I hate their fighting. It used to scare me. Now it just makes me mad. I don't like to be around it., but I have to live with it. Seems like Dad is always irritated at something. I get sick of it. He can't say anything nice most of the time.

"What do they want from me? Whatever it is, I can't give it. Ever. Whatever it is, it isn't me. Ever. No point in trying. What's it going to get me? Nuthin'. If he is going to be mad at me all the time, I'm just going to be mad right back. He isn't so tough. Spare me the lecture.

"I don't always wake up mad, just mostly. I'd rather stay asleep. School is as bad as home. A big-assed teacher telling me what to do. So I get in trouble. I try to figure out how I can skip 'cause I'd just as soon be anywhere but there. I do not do homework. Let's get that straight. Why should I? Like I'm going to walk out on the stage with all those prisses and get my homework award? I don't think so. Save it for somebody in the band. Anyway, I make them yell at me 25 times before I get out of bed. Then I take my sweet time. Wow, do they get ripped. You should see. Sometimes I wake up and ask myself, 'How can I ruin their day today?' I can always come up with something. Most other times it just happens whether I want it to or not. If they'd just leave me alone I'd be okay. They think they can tell me what to do. Right. We'll see.

> "Sometimes I wake up and ask myself, 'How can I ruin their day today?' I can always come up with something. Most other times it just happens whether I want it to or not."

"My Mom says, 'You know we love you?' Huh? Who is we? If that is what love is, I'm not buying. Wish I had a real set of parents, parents that don't fight. One of my buddies has nice parents. I think about moving in with him sometimes. They seem okay although my buddy gives them a lot of grief. I don't know why. They seem alright to me. I'd switch with him if I could. He has a snotty older sister, but I could cope.

"Know what I do with their love? Push it in their face, see how much they like listening to that garbage. Then I take off. Go someplace. Do something. Anything not to be around them. I don't give them an inch. Every time I do, every time I relax a little bit and try to be nice, something happens and they always say, 'There you go again.'

"I can't win. It is like they expect me to get in trouble. I can't escape it. So I don't try much. Never works when I do. I do what they think I'm gonna do; get thrown off the bus or something.

"I think a lot. I think more than other kids, too. I'm sure of that. I don't think much about the hard stuff. Feels yucky. I think about what I'm going to do next, like 10 seconds from now. And then I do it. It can be fun. Going slow doesn't feel right. It's like I'm giving in to my folks. Why would I do that? What did they do to deserve it?

"They say, 'You know we have rules in this house, young man.' Oh, yeah? Show me one that isn't bullshit. I like it when they make one of those refrigerator charts. 'These are the rules,' they say. 'If you follow them, we'll give you a quarter.' Whoopie. A quarter? They think they can make me do what they want for a quarter? They don't have enough money to make me do what they want. They don't have enough anything. I'll do what I want, when I want and there is nothing they can do about it. Whatever it is, it sure won't be on one of their charts.

"They think they can control me. Their twinky therapist tells them to put boundaries around me. Is that a riot or what? If they'd just look around, they would see they can't. I can match anything they do. I'm not about to roll over and play dead. Do they think I'm nuts or something? This isn't about being a good boy. Like I said, I can do it. I just don't plan on doing it soon."

## Spike talks about family

"I've got a family, such as it is. There is the hopeless Angelique, my Mom, Dad, and Ruff. Ruff is special. He makes up for a lot. But that's it.

"I don't think we have a normal family, though. Normal families do normal things, like ones on TV. They laugh. They hang out. You never see them angry, at least not for real. If they do, it doesn't take long before they get all sappy and huggy. Life is good again. It isn't real. What I live in is real.

"In my family, we don't get sappy or huggy, and life is never good again. Somebody is always angry at somebody. Always. Somebody gets mad at somebody, and off we go. It gets out of control real fast.

"Dinner time is probably the worst. Nobody wants it. It is hard to eat. Somebody comes to the table pissed. You can tell. They are really quiet. It doesn't take much to get the fumes to blow up.

"Then somebody says, 'I'm not going to eat here. I can't stand it.'

"And somebody else says, 'Good, so don't. I don't care.'

> "In my family, we don't get sappy or huggy, and life is never good again. Somebody is always angry at somebody. Always. Somebody gets mad at somebody, and off we go."

"I'd rather not come down to it at all, so I drag my feet. It makes them mad. They end up blaming it on me which is only a little true and then I have to get tough myself and tell them to get fucked, at which point Dad freaks and threatens me. But I don't take it. I give it right back.

"Lousy dinner all in all. They'd be better off not to have dinner. It never works. I think somebody told them that we're supposed to have family dinners. Whoever said that never saw my family. It's stupid. We never seem to get around to the part where you ask everyone how their day went. Who cares? It was probably shitty anyway.

"You think dinner is a problem? You should see us at the holidays. Dinner is just a warm up. I hate the holidays. First, we all have to go get the tree. They never get the one I want—a giant one—so I just stay in the car. Then we get it home and drag it into the house. Then we fight over decorations. Somebody says, 'NO! It doesn't go that way.'

"And then somebody else says, 'I'll do it any way I want.'

"Then somebody else says, 'Why do you always have to be such a moron?'

"Followed by somebody saying, 'Fine…do the goddamned thing yourself.'

"It's the same every year. And that's just the tree. Then we have presents sitting under the tree. Somebody always wants to spoil it by pulling off some of the wrapping paper to see what's inside. Actually, I tend to be that 'somebody'.

"If I see that one more time, I'm canceling Christmas, and it's all going back to the store!"

"On Christmas Eve? Get real. Then there is coming down stairs at 5am on Christmas morning and finding absolutely nothing I want. What a jip!

"Then there is Christmas dinner. We used to go to relatives', but there was always trouble. Now we invite either Mom or Dad's relatives to our house. Not much of an improvement, if you ask me. Hard to say which is worse. Either brings their boring stupid kids. I don't want them into my stuff so I push them out of my room and slam the door. They get the idea but I also get some door pounding by my Dad who tells me I'm a selfish brat and why don't I grow up. He is just thumping his chest for the relatives. Big deal. I doubt they are impressed. Who cares?

"Between stupid presents and stupid relatives, it's a pretty stupid day. The dinner part is over as soon as I can make it over.

"'Do you have to eat like such a pig? Sit up!'

"I don't hang around the table any longer than it takes to get full. I take off and find one of my friends. Mom is generally crying by now anyway. Dad is angry again. My sister…oh, who knows. My friends may not be much, but they are an improvement over what I have to live with."

## What Spike Thinks About Love

"Love means everybody is happy.

"We don't do love in my family. Love is when your parents tuck you in at night. You slide through the sheets and snuggle in. Then your Mom and Dad kiss you goodnight. Nobody kisses me goodnight. I probably wouldn't let 'em.

> "We don't do love in my family. Love is when your parents tuck you in at night. You slide through the sheets and snuggle in. Then your Mom and Dad kiss you goodnight."

"Or love is when everybody climbs onto Dad's lap and he reads a story. I think about the last place I am going to climb onto is Dad's lap, not that he is offering or anything. The story thing isn't going anywhere anyway. It wouldn't work.

"I love Ruff, but I don't think anybody loves anybody else. He doesn't criticize me, and I don't criticize him. Maybe if he could talk he would, but I doubt it. We understand each other. Maybe Angelique loves somebody, but she is hopeless anyway. My folks don't love each other. Not really.

"Love means you are nice. Love means you aren't on somebody's case. Love means you aren't worried about what is coming next. Whatever is next is probably bad. You have to be ready to fight, at least I am. I hate surprises. Surprises mean something has gone wrong. I don't mind surprising everybody else, I just don't like it when they do it to me. So, I'm always ready.

"Love means you can screw up and nobody notices. Everybody notices mistakes where I live and they let you know. It is hard to find a place to hide. That's why I take off a lot.

"Love means that you want to be with someone special, and they want to be with you. It's when your parents hold hands and whisper to each other. Or they say, 'Hi, Honey, I'm home. What's for dinner?'

"My Dad wouldn't say that. Mom would tell him dinner was whatever she was cooking and as for the 'Hi, Honey' part, she'd think he was nuts. They don't talk that way. I don't think anyone feels very special where I live. Not me, anyway.

"The yelling that goes on in this place gives me headaches. I get them every week. If I don't skip school 'cause I feel like shit, I get sent home 'cause they find me throwing up in the bathroom. The nurse calls my Dad. She puts me on the phone with him. 'You okay?' he'd say.

'Yeah,' I'd say.

"'I'll be there in a few minutes. You gonna wait for me?'

"'Yeah.' If I'm really sick, I wait. Otherwise, I take off when the nurse leaves the room, headache or no headache.

"We went to my Grandma's for dinner last Sunday. I don't think she looks forward to these little visits. Don't know why my folks bother. It has been a while since we did it. She's pretty old. It went okay. No more anger than normal, I suppose.

"When I get there, I just go to Grandma's TV room and watch a game from the moment we get there 'til the moment we leave. My Mom doesn't even beg me to come to the table.

"I used to love my Grandma. I don't know what got into me, I must have rocks for brains, but I went up to her afterwords while she was standing there washing dishes and asked her, 'Do you love me?'

## How it Feels to Be a Victim

"Want to know what it feels like being a loser? It feels like crap. You are the lowest of the low. Everybody is better than you are—better looking, smarter, more popular, everything. You also feel alone. Really alone. If there is anything out there that is bad, it will happen to you, 'cause you deserve it. And there is nothing to make it easier. There is something about you that makes all the shit happen.

> "Want to know what it feels like being a loser? It feels like crap. You are the lowest of the low. Everybody is better than you are—better looking, smarter, more popular, everything."

"Then they stick you in a 'special' class. In what way is this supposed to make me feel 'special?' Only if stupid is special. Where do they get some of these names? Even if you aren't in a 'special' class, you are treated as if you should be. It makes me want to hit somebody.

"It's like you also have this sign around your neck saying 'I'm Trouble—Stay Away.'"

"What it means is that nobody can handle me, which I think is kinda funny. It's also kinda not funny. You get shoved down the stairs a lot. Not that I don't do my share of shoving right back again. You bet I do. But you get shoved in more ways than one. You end up in the principal's office where they call your parents, like that's gonna help anything. Or you get suspended. There are worse things than that. And you get all the rejects for your buddies. There are some strange ones out there. It beats being alone, I guess. At least they understand the rules. And I don't get to sit at the popular table in the lunchroom. Well, who cares?

"I don't put up with any of this without a fight. It isn't fair. Not a bit of it. Why should I? I don't see anybody riding to my rescue.

"Fact of the matter is, though, I haven't hit anybody in a while. I can. They all know I can. I just haven't. I've even let a couple chances slide. I get tired of all the noise. I may let you get away with being just an ordinary asshole. If you are a big asshole, that's different. Depends on how I feel mostly.

"Speaking of assholes, I don't like getting on the bus in the morning. I don't like getting off 30 minutes later either. Assuming, of course, that they allow me on the bus in the first place. The bus driver hates me. School cuts into my sleep. It isn't worth the effort it takes to get there. Something is always waiting for me. Something I'd just as soon not deal with.

"Sometimes I wonder where all this came from, or how I'm on the bottom. It's hard to see. My parents are my parents. Kind of stuck there. Most teachers aren't worth the effort it takes to be nice to them. So, sometimes, I'm not. Every once in a while, you come across one that doesn't think you're a total waste.

"A lot of them yell as much as my folks do. I never noticed before. And they are so nasty sarcastic. It stinks. Or they like to ridicule you in front of other kids, like that's gonna make me behave. I hate most of them.

"If I could bring Ruff to school, the day would probably go better. Ruff calms me down. That's what my parents should do: find me a school to go to where I can take Ruff. What a great idea. Then I could get out of that dump. I sometimes think I could be one of those kids that brings a gun to school, 'cept I don't have one.

> "Some days I'd like to get on my bike and ride away. If I could just leave everything behind, things would be better. But I don't know how to make it work."

"I wish I could start over. Maybe move someplace where when ol' Spike comes down the hall, they don't whisper. Some days I'd like to get on my bike and ride away. If I could just leave everything behind, things would be better. But I don't know how to make it work. I don't know how I'd eat or where I'd sleep. I'm kinda stuck there, too.

"I'll have to settle for my fort. I doesn't take me very far. I built it next to the garage. There is just room for Ruff and me. I made it out of pallets with some roofing I swiped. The door has a spring latch with a lock on the inside. I've stayed out there in my sleeping bag. I bring a couple sandwiches. It's okay. Assuming we don't move again, it's okay. If we do move, I'll burn the damn thing to the ground along with the garage. I'm not sharing.

"Forgive? Me? This is a joke, right?

"One day, I get a phone call. Well, my Dad does. He gives the phone to me. It's this guy at the college. He says he wants to interview me. I say, 'Whatcha gonna give me if I do?' He said, 'Five bucks.' I said, 'Okay.' I went to the college. It was just him and me. We talk about this and that. Finally, he says, 'Spike, have you ever thought about forgiving your folks?'

"I'm like, 'Are you kidding?'

"'No,' he says.

"'That's the dumbest thing I ever heard.'

"'Why?' he wonders.

"I said, 'It just is.'

"'Do you like them?'

"'No, should I?' I said.

"Then, he says, 'Most kids like their folks.'

"'I'm not most kids.'

"'Are you angry with them?' he asks.

"'What do you think?' I said.

"And he's like, 'Do you love them?'

"So I said, 'I think I need to get out of here....'

"What is this guy, Mr. Question? I got my $5. He told me he hoped I'd come back. I said maybe I would, maybe I wouldn't. But as for the forgiving thing, I didn't know what to tell him other than NO. He wants me to forgive. Amazing. They never asked me to forgive them, not that I would have listened. I'd like to know what they think they did wrong that they need me to forgive. I think they are up to something.

"Life sucks. My parents suck right along with it. Kids are kids, like we matter. Everything rolls downhill. There I am at the bottom and—whamo!—I get mowed over. And, they want me to say it's okay? I don't think so.

"This being knocked flat is nothing I looked for. I suppose they didn't stick pins in me on purpose, the way you pin a butterfly in summer camp, a 'special' camp, by the way. But how would I know? I think it probably feels about the same. But I don't know either. I don't know why it happened, once you get down to it. I'm a kid. How am I supposed to know? All I know is that life with them is awful, makes me want to hide.

> "Life sucks. My parents suck right along with it. Kids are kids, like we matter. Everything rolls downhill. There I am at the bottom and—whamo!—I get mowed over."

"But forgive? I can't pretend this shit never happened 'cause it did. And it isn't as if I am going to forget 'cause I won't.

"The school is still on my back. I still want to choke Angelique every time I lay eyes on her. I still spend my life looking to piss off my parents. I sleep with one eye open. Doesn't feel like much is new. I should ask Ruff how he feels about the idea.

"I haven't liked them for the longest time, though part of me wants to like them. I don't let on. Whatever they want, I want something else. I know how to piss them off. I'm good at it, too. Real good. I know everybody thinks I'm the problem. That's just the way it is. I'm hard to get along with but I don't care because they piss me off. I have to fight.

"Anyway, the day I wake up and don't feel like everyone's pin cushion is the day I might decide to be nice. I think that is about as close to forgiveness as I can get. I can't see it so I'm not planning any parties. But, you know what? They want me to stop first. Who are they kidding? They're hopeless. They pull this shit on me day after day, and I am supposed to be the one to quit first? Brother.

"I was real glad when they started going to the shrink. I thought 'Yippee!' At least I don't have to go along, though, as I said, they tried to get me to go. 'I'm already special enough,' I said."

"For the last time, GET OUTTA BED! You'll be late!"

# CHAPTER 4 : Spike's Story

## The Experts Take a Look at Spike—What Makes Spike Abnormal?

Five experts were consulted on Spike's inability to be happy. They looked at him from five different perspectives: character development, family, love, victimization, and forgiveness. Parents should compare their own child to Spike. There probably are some parallels. Importantly, these five areas change as parents work their way through P.A.C.T. These are representations of where Spike is now. Parents who complete P.A.C.T. should reread this chapter and see how much their child has changed by comparison. It will be reassuring.

### Spike's Character

Let's see if we can understand what makes Spike tick and what his present says about his future.

- The motivation for parents to invest themselves in P.A.C.T. is divided between Spike's today and his tomorrow.
- We will discuss five building blocks of happiness: character development, family, love, victimization, and forgiveness.
- Making sense of these is essential to promoting a stable, useful life.

First, there is the matter of character. Psychiatrist Liane Leedom, MD, in her book, *Just Like His Father?* notes that we have a built-in guidance device she calls an 'inner triangle.'

- Ideally, the inner triangle consists of equal parts love, impulse, and morals.
- The three elements play off one another and keep us balanced.
- They constitute our 'character,' a quality that distinguishes us from one another.

Spike has character. You may not like it, but he has one.

- His character doesn't mesh well with others, but he couldn't be human without one of some kind.
- He does not have love, impulse and morals in equal amounts as other children do.

Spike's character got derailed. He once had the beginnings of normal character (or a normal triangle).
- Its development got damaged by his unhappiness.
- Damage to one part of the triangle can't be made up by other sides.
- His attempt to compensate will look like limping.
- Damage takes a long time to repair.
- In short, Spike has a character deficiency.

## Love

The first part of character is love. People who don't love easily don't form attachments easily. Humans don't do well as isolates. They need attachments. Spike can love but loving a dog is not the same thing as loving a human.

> He understands that like/love is how people judge him. If it weren't for the constant fear he feels, he would act on liking and loving himself. Spike is too scared to love. His parents need to fix that.

- Everyone in Spike's life is either expendable or Spike says he despises them.
- Ruff fills some of the love hole in Spike's life.
- Since he doesn't love people, he manipulates. His relationships are exploitative. There is little give and take.
- He needs more dependence with his family.
- Families exist to shape children. Spike has rejected shaping by his family. He intends to shape himself, but it won't work. He is not ready to flee the nest. He is still a child.
- A consequence of poor attachment is a need to dominate. Spike wants control.
- So, we have a controlling child who doesn't form attachments easily, who is inappropriately independent and exploitative.
- This child is in trouble. Is he doomed? No. Will he struggle? Yes, and everyone around him will struggle too.

His parents won't believe it now, but as they go through P.A.C.T. Spike will show that he wants to be both liked and loved. He understands that like/love is how people judge him. If it weren't for the constant fear he feels, he would act on liking and loving himself. Spike is too scared to love. His parents need to fix that.

## Morals

Then there is the problem of morals. Morals are a set of rules, but Spike doesn't like rules. He doesn't like having anyone tell him what to do.

- Morals are rules that distinguish between what is yours and what is his.
- Spike figures everything is his. He feels entitled.

- Fairness is a big deal to Spike, but his sense of fairness is broken. Fairness is give and take. Spike takes.
- Spike's parents are sure that he is amoral. He isn't, but you wouldn't know that to see him.
- Spike seems stuck at some earlier, more child-like level of functioning. Is it temporary? In large part, yes.
- It takes time and effort to move from the risky fringes of life back into the great gray middle. The world does not run black and white. It runs on gray.
- People can afford to stray to the edges once in a while if they are comfortable with gray.
- Comfort with grey is 'good adjustment,' whereas comfort with black and white is 'bad adjustment.'

Spike gradually learns that 'bad' is a waste of time. He learns it while his parents learn P.A.C.T. The waste of time bought him only isolation and constant judgment.

## Impulse

Lastly, we have impulse. The problem with impulse is knowing when to act and when not to act.

- Spike doesn't live beyond today. He grabs when something floats by.
- He acts on his various drives for pleasure and postpones nothing. He will rarely work for a thing.
- Spike hasn't much in the way of inhibition and he has no reason to delay anything.
- Spike figures he has more to lose by postponing than by grabbing.
- He may not know much about himself, but he knows that if he relaxes, the world will run right over him.
- As Spike responds to the work his parents do in P.A.C.T., it will show up in his impulse control. He will moderate his impulses for them. It is a gift.
- They will know it is a gift. Their son will seem newly cautious about life.
- He will take longer to do whatever everyone else gets done sooner. He will be more hesitant, more deliberate. It will be a big change.

Spike will be more fearful than previously. 'Fear' was rarely used in the same sentence as 'Spike.' What is Spike fearing? Failure. He also fears a return to the bad old days of being out of control. Ironically, he was doing his best to look like he was in control. Yet, fear won't be his principal motivator. The motivator is pleasing his folks and the fear of disappointing them, as far-fetched as they think that may be.

Good character development requires that normally developing people need all three sides of the triangle—love, morals, impulse. The triangle is dynamic; it stretches in and out.

- Most of us have powerful incentives to keep the angles even and connected to one another.

- Spike can get them back in alignment, but it will be hard. It may be the hardest job of his life. He needs a model.
- He will have to fight against himself to create the model.
- He doesn't have one. His parents are working at it.
- He is left to his own devices to construct his model.

He is essentially presented with a blob of clay and told to produce himself. It is hard to make progress when he does his "Mirror, mirror on the wall…" routine and sees a loser.

Spike's character is a reflection of his parents' character.

- Spike can't see that his parents are struggling to reset their own models. He is a child. All he sees is his own resentment.
- His parents have a deficiency in impulse. If they can resolve this, it will be because of him. Their sense of love has taken a battering, but still exists. Their morals are skewed as well.
- They spent an inordinate amount of time blaming him before they came to see that they had a role.

If there were serious problems—like addictive behavior or anti-social tendencies—their ability to adjust themselves would be more challenging. The more symptoms of mental disturbance the parent has, the more difficult the odyssey through P.A.C.T.

The way his parents respond to P.A.C.T. will make a big difference in Spike's subsequent character development.

- Dr. Leedom's thesis is that Spike was either genetically predestined to be the Spike we know and love, or that the circumstances of his life turned an otherwise blank slate into four feet of fury.
- Which one applies to Spike will become apparent as his parents progress through P.A.C.T. and Spike reacts to their progress.
- If all goes well in P.A.C.T., we parents will learn that, intentionally or not, we merely were looking in the wrong direction. This doesn't mean we created Spike's problems but it doesn't mean we caught them early either.
- If all does not go well, we can have some faith that our forebears gave us a foul genetic stew that we were left to cope with.
- One thing is clear: it didn't have to get this bad. Genetic stew or not, parents can act. Spike has given out signals for years.
- We have been trained to look at the awful child and say, "It's the child's problem; it is the child who has to get over it." Actually, that is partially true.
- Spike has to cope with whatever cards he has been dealt. Our job as parents, since we missed the at-risk signals, is to get out of the way. It just took us a long time to recognize that we were stumbling over our own parental feet.

Don't feel too badly. There aren't any parents who successfully complete P.A.C.T. who haven't smacked themselves on the forehead and said, "I shoulda done this five years ago." And, there are a lot more who don't care enough for their child to learn it in the first place. **Learning P.A.C.T. is an act of love.**

## Family

Spike's unhappiness is not a random event, according to John Bradshaw's *The Family*. Bradshaw says that children like Spike come from dysfunctional families. Nobody wants to be dysfunctional, but lots of us are. Practically no one is spared.

- Just about everyone's character formation is compromised by their family. Everyone's capacity to love is stifled.
- Problems with character and love don't mean that we don't function at all; it means we limp. One or more of our cylinders aren't firing.
- We get up in the morning, shower, have breakfast, and end up swearing at our child.
- Dysfunction means we function poorly. Is there divorce? Is there emotional disturbance? Is there an out-of-control child in your family? Then there is dysfunction. Dysfunction is as common as rain in Seattle.

Dysfunctional families may be the rule, not the exception. It is a testament to our flexibility as humans that we can be quite seriously flawed and still make it through life. Even if a family didn't start off as dysfunctional, it ends up that way with a child like Spike.

Dysfunction is one of the clichés of our time. Get past the cliché. Dysfunction is real. It governs how Spike happened in the first place. It governs how he is likely to function over time. Spikes tend to happen in families where dysfunction is generational.

> It is a testament to our flexibility as humans that we can be quite seriously flawed and still make it through life. Even if a family didn't start off as dysfunctional, it ends up that way with a child like Spike.

- There is probably a genetic component to Spike's history. Our genes tend to incline us one way or the other.
- There is also a teaching component. Spikes are taught by their families how to be unhappy. We teach others how to treat us.
- Outrageous as it may seem, we have taught Spike how to treat us and how he should treat others. This part hurts. No one wants to own it. Fortunately, what you teach, you can unteach.
- You are beginning to understand that how you have coped with Spike has maintained his unhappiness.
- It may ease the pain a bit to learn that the teaching wasn't deliberate.
- The good news is that much about this generational cycle can be stopped. We can teach children a different way to treat us and, by extension, how they should treat others.

In order to stop the dysfunction, family members must recognize symptoms. They must get past their need to deny dysfunction. They must do what you are doing. Denial is a powerful inhibitor to change. Following P.A.C.T. makes it easy to see ourselves and makes it easy to stop denying.

Spike thrives on our denial. Getting past denial is so much better if it happens before we have children.

- There are plenty of at-risk signals.
- It is only when we have children and those children encounter rough patches that some of us can risk taking a look at ourselves.
- Not all children react the same way to family dysfunction.
- We may or may not see our own dysfunction played out in a child.

A child with a predisposition, genetic or otherwise, may react badly if circumstances warrant.

Spike had many at-risk behaviors that didn't get noticed. His character developed accordingly. P.A.C.T. acknowledges the at-risk behaviors in a very round about way. Therapy goes after them more directly. Both avenues are useful and reinforce one another. Bradshaw lists them (with P.A.C.T. paraphrasing):

- ✗ Self-control–Self-control is heavily stressed in Spike's family. They do it in public so well it blocks out feelings and emotions. They control themselves so well they explode. They don't see the lit fuse. Spike holds the match. It's his role. But they don't control themselves well in private.
- ✗ Right vs. wrong–Spike's folks are always right. When Spike is wrong, which he thinks is all the time, he is not merely wrong, he is blamed and shamed. Being right in Spike's family is competitive. Somebody keeps score. The competition is too much for Spike.
- ✗ Criticizing–Spike's parents blame him through criticism. It's one way they keep control. It is also a way for them to avoid seeing the shame of failure that they commit in their own lives.
- ✗ Denial–Spike is encouraged to deny how he sees, hears, feels, and thinks. He is encouraged to see, hear, feel, and think the family way. The family way is better. His way is inferior and wrong.
- ✗ Perfectionism–Spike's family is perfect (or at least perfect enough) and if he can't see it, he is just grumpy, irritable, selfish, or a troublemaker. Family imperfections are all in his head. He shouldn't talk about them in any event.
- ✗ Defensive–Since Spike's family is perfect, any hint of criticism is preparation for argument, not a means for understanding. Spike is told he is selfish or rude whenever he objects.
- ✗ Open-ended conflict–Conflicts in Spike's family are never concluded. They go on through never-ending argument or through a silent agreement to avoid some subjects.
- ✗ Independence–Spike's folks only trust themselves. They stress self-sufficiency and independence. They either wall themselves off from some people or go the other way and

enmesh themselves. They are either aloof or incomplete, but they never get their basic needs met either way, nor do their children. Think about this for a minute. The list is telling you several things:

- Communication, both verbal and non-verbal, is poor.
- Honesty doesn't exist.
- Energy is wasted maintaining fictions about the family.
- Spike exists as the foil to all of it.
- Spike's function in the family is to be the jerk.

Spike's parents would be aghast to admit his role. He certainly is obliging them whether they do or not. The above list are things you may need to ponder more deeply.

- Rip the list out of this book.
- Take it to a therapist.
- Tell him or her that you are a survivor of a dysfunctional family, that you have produced a dysfunctional child of your own, that you are in P.A.C.T. to do something about it and would like help.
- Tell him or her that you may have inadvertently stuck a pin in your child's inner triangle and you want to reinflate it. (You may need to explain what that means).

You don't know it yet, but this process will introduce you to the concept of forgiveness. Forgiveness is at the heart of banishing dysfunction. But first you must admit the dysfunction. Admission often requires the help of another.

Spike's parents are not monsters. In fact, they are nice people. You'd like them. You'd probably invite them over for drinks. You would have to know what you were looking for to see the dysfunction in this family. Spike's parents are skilled at seeming whole, happy, and pleasant. In fact, they are so skilled that they have convinced themselves that they are whole, happy, and pleasant.

Family matters:

- It matters in character formation.
- It matters in love which is the squishiest, yet the most important of all subjects.
- In fact, family love is so important that if something happens to our family, the state will try to find us another or we will try to find a replacement family on our own.

We need people who care about us. However, many families chug along without all caring cylinders operating. We get used to the pings and, over time, think they are normal.

There is, by the way, no requirement that P.A.C.T. users accept the dysfunction thesis. They can get a great deal of change just using the program. They are likely to get more by figuring out what, if any, role dysfunction plays in the life of their family.

## Love

We already know that character formation is inevitable. What we don't know is whether the character is anything we'd want to invite over to dinner. We need encouragement to maintain all the effort we will marshal on Spike's behalf. So we will look a bit further at love.

Care to calculate the love Spike and his family have toward one another?

- On the surface, Ruff aside, not much looks loving.
- Spike is caught up in his need to be angry.
- He is so absorbed in his feelings of misery, that he can scarcely say a nice thing to anyone, much less offer an expression of love.

His parents, while they are often annoyed or worse, remind themselves to sound nicer and act nicer. But his sister would gleefully flush Spike down the toilet.

Yet, if we do a little digging we can find foundations of love. The foundation tentatively anchors this family together and gives us some hope that all the work done on behalf of Spike will make a difference.

First, the fact that they bother to fight at all is significant. If fighting were missing, they'd be out of business. We only fight with people that matter. Fighting shows a level of commitment. However, since fighting threatens to tear the family apart, we can't take too much comfort in it.

Some love is conditional and can be temporary. A marriage, for instance, can start in love but can end in divorce. Fortunately for Spike, family love differs from marital love.

Second, measurable love actually exists in this family. Sternberg's *Triangular Theory of Love* is a good standard by which to measure Spike's family. Sternberg says love consists of three elements: **intimacy** (a need to share), **passion** (a need to desire which may or may not be sexual), and **commitment** (a need to maintain a relationship). Love of family requires them all. We expect the most from family, so we tend to both want and give the most. Each family member contributes something.

## Spike and the triangle

We know Spike understands love; after all, he has Ruff. Ruff is a surrogate for a human as well as an adored object. Ruff fills a need temporarily. Spike's interactions with Ruff suggest intimacy because there are shared feelings between the two. He displays both a desire to be with Ruff and commitment to the relationship that will endure. Spike's passion is evident in the thrill he gets when he comes home to Ruff. All the barking, tail-wagging, bouncing up and down, and slobbering have their purposes. There is nothing quite like bulldog slobber to signify commitment.

All of this is important because if we could not find scraps of love in Spike's life, we'd have reason to be seriously worried about his future. We should, instead, only be moderately worried.

## Angelique and the triangle

What can we say? She is perfect. She shares what she has with her parents whom she mostly likes though she has her moments of resentment. In a weak moment, she will even share with Spike. And, in another weak moment, he will actually let her. She looks forward to her parents coming into her room and saying good night. She commits to them easily. She likes those few minutes with them when they read her a story. Life with Spike has made her independent. She can't depend on her parents to be available to her since they are always tied up with him.

She seems content, at least from a distance. Still waters run deep and we may have an opportunity to witness a profound anger in Angelique that comes with living with someone who doesn't contribute to the family's need for love. Spike sucks out far more oxygen than he puts back.

## Dad and the triangle

Dad doesn't say a whole lot. Expressions of affection are not his thing. He'd rather show than say. He doesn't do much of either. In fact, he is angry a lot. He knows he is angry and doesn't like it. He feels trapped. Going to work is a relief. He looks forward to his friends on the weekend. There is tension between he and his wife. She is on him a lot about what he did and didn't do. Somehow it always centers on Spike. He stopped sharing with Spike because it was so unrewarding. His wife says he should keep trying. He tries but his trying always ends in shouting. He knows Angelique can be sweet, and he feels guilty about not being able to provide her a normal home. He takes pleasure in her success in school, her friends and her outlook.

He sometimes wonders, though, why he hangs around. He doesn't seem to fulfill much of any function, hasn't got much authority, and doesn't know where any of this is headed. It is hard to evaluate Dad's love. His commitment flags now and again. There is precious little intimacy of any kind. And passion? What's that? Is that the part where he yells? His love is there even if it doesn't jump out. But it probably needs to jump out.

> She is just as assertive about being a Mom in a difficult situation as her husband is resigned in the same situation. Neither approach seems productive. And, significantly, neither of them are on the same page.

## Mom and the triangle

Mom sure tries. Hauling children here and there. Baking cookies. Organizing this and that. Spike is mean to her, but he will subvert much that she does. But, she doesn't give up. She is of the "Bulldozer School of Impaired Child Relationships" which says that you keep pushing ahead no matter what. Her pushing riles Spike, and he ends up cursing her. She just won't quit. Her need for her children to respond to her is never in doubt. She is passionate about her family to a fault. Literally.

She is just as assertive about being a Mom in a difficult situation as her husband is resigned in the same situation. Neither approach seems productive. And, significantly, neither of them are on the same page.

Feel the love? Probably not. You'd have to look for it.

- This family functions on a thin diet of love.
- How well any of them functions on the Love Triangle of intimacy, passion, and commitment is subjective. They all are somewhere on the scale. They give what they have, but sometimes it isn't much.
- The children, being children, are spontaneous with their feelings while parents tend to fret.
- The environment is barely congenial. It is more apt to punish demonstrations of love than reward them as love is treated skeptically.
- Every day is not somebody's birthday. There isn't much to celebrate anyway.

But the scene could be worse. Everyone feels sufficient commitment to the other to make the struggle through P.A.C.T. possible. Their passions are more often than not seen in their anger, but at least it is something. There isn't much intimacy. It is hard to warm up to someone who is disappointed in you.

Is Spike lucky in love? Spike is lucky to make his home in this biological family. He isn't being raised by grandparents, by foster parents, or by adoptive parents. The connection is more tentative in non-bio parent settings. A biological bond is associated with success, not merely with the program but with something even more basic: staying together.

It is the exceptional non-bio parent family that can weather a seriously unhappy child. A non-bio parent family is much more likely to give up. There can be too many deficiencies in intimacy, passion, or commitment. Even in those instances where the father leaves the family due to pressure, the family still exists.

Of the three indicators—love, passion, and commitment—we can generally assume that commitment is far less well established in non-biological families. The vulnerability of commitment threatens passion and intimacy.

Love equals attachment. Intimacy, passion, and commitment are the constituents of attachment.

- Attachment is just 'love' with more letters.
- Love is such a soft word and experimenters gravitate to its synonym: attachment.
- Spike's family is attached to one another but the attachment varies.
- There are biological families in which lack of attachment is a serious problem. These families probably have members whose genetic makeup makes attachment difficult or impossible.
- Such families have members who are sociopathic and, thus, can never attach well.
- That is not the case in this family. The family is attached sufficiently to keep trying.
- If they are successful in P.A.C.T., it will only be because attachment via intimacy, passion and commitment kept them focused.
- The nice thing about attachment is that its constituents are hard to eliminate. They all can grow, too.

A lot of the love in this family is actually latent. Greater expressions of love will pop out as the parents get better about handling their disappointment and anger, and become more effective parents. It will be a happy surprise.

## Victimization
### What's a victim?

- A victim is both a fact and a state of mind that must be overcome.
- A victim is somebody who feels like a victim; they are injured and feel blamed and alone.
- How they got that way may be irrelevant; injury comes from sources great and small.
- Victims feel shame; shame predicts how people function.

Spike sees himself as a victim. He is blamed by everyone. His sense of shame is degrading. It makes him angry. He is isolated and alone even when he is in a group. His life has been one drama after the next.

Spike's parents also see themselves as victims, injured by him, blamed, shamed by everyone else and all alone to ponder what they did to deserve it.

- They say no one understands what they go through, how they feel or what they need.
- Their feelings of victimization predict how they will function.
- They are humiliated by the experience and often angry.

Their tolerance for their domestic dramas predicts how soon they will fight back effectively. The producer of the dramas is Spike. Some Spike brings on himself. The drama gets old, especially when it produces so little.

Blame cuts both ways. We are a victim if we can find something to blame. We can't have one without the other. The other is the perpetrator. It's not a nice word, and it conjures up ugliness. But if that is the way that Spike sees us, then that is the way Spike sees us. The reverse, however, is also true.

Parents are likely to look at Spike and see someone who is making hash of their lives. The cycle of recrimination goes on forever. A lifetime of finger pointing only results in wasted opportunity.

Too much energy is spent convincing ourselves and others that we are victims.

- Depending on how serious our feeling of victimization, we may decide that we need to do something about it
- We struggle to insulate ourselves from change until we can't stand it any more.
- Parents blame children for turning their lives upside down; children blame their parents for allowing them to be out of control.
- Both can hang on to their feelings for years.
- If we can convincingly blame others and feel bitter, we feel relieved of the obligation to do something about the feelings, except, of course, complain.

There is nothing like a dose of victimhood to give us a rush of virtue. The rush, however, feels good only briefly. Once it and the accompanying self-pity starts to wear, it's time to create change.

We haven't much patience for victims, especially if we can't see a smoking gun. There is little understanding out there which means we won't get much sympathy. Sooner or later, the self-pity will sound hollow.

P.A.C.T. doesn't say parents shouldn't feel the way they feel; it says continuing to feel that way will do them no good. They need to put wraps on their own childhood experiences and make themselves available to their children in a way that will help children develop well.

We can't just tell Spike to give up his feelings. He isn't likely to listen any better than his parents, although the feelings are often mutual. We can, however, create the conditions that Spike can use to deal with feelings effectively.

The feelings of victimization wear thin. If Spike grows to adulthood and still complains about his tough childhood, he could insist that it retarded his ability to advance in life.

- We are responsible for our actions. There is no escape.
- Defendant attempts to invoke the traumas of their childhoods, as reason why they should not be held responsible for criminal acts, rarely succeed.
- A lifetime of spousal or child abuse may get the abuser's mattress doused in kerosene and set aflame with the abuser still on it, but the abusee is probably still going to jail.

We all have to accept the conditions of our life, even abuse, if we are going to make a workable life out of the pieces given to us. Some can do it. Some can't.

Continued blaming postpones change. We can hide for a while behind genetic determinism all we want, but someday we need to make things better.

- Legions of the disabled have learned to compensate. Parents can, too.
- To be stuck in victimhood is to be stuck in a closed loop.
- Energy is expended maintaining our sense of victimization as we rehearse our miseries.
- At one level, this is coping.
- At another level, it is wasting time because the closed loop is filled with self-judgments which are as damning as the judgments of others.

It doesn't matter whether those miseries are minor or major. Only Spike can plot his own escape. No one can do it for him. The best Spike's parents can do is clear a path out of the woods. Spike has to walk it himself.

To be stuck in victimhood is to be stuck in fear. Giving up self-judgment and not listening to the judgments of others requires an act of bravery that not all are ready for.

- Fear of being successful is powerful.
- The comfort of the well-worn rut, albeit the home of a loser, may be preferable to the risk involved in becoming something else.

When and if the rut becomes intolerable, the victim will start to climb out. To be stuck in victimhood is to practice self-deceit. Recovery requires awareness. Awareness requires honesty. And honesty is no fun. It is, however, essential.

- Honesty does not mean telling everyone what we think of them. This kind of honesty is mostly mean.
- Honesty really suggests the self-appraisal of personal weaknesses as well as strengths, and doing something about the former.
- Don't like the rut? Climb out.
- What is it about the rut that gets under your skin? Its unremitting negativity? Probably.

Don't like what negativity says about you, your family, your life? The negativity has probably become a frame of mind. You can't just will it away.

Working P.A.C.T. will make a big difference in attitude because whatever negative tapes you continue to play in your head, you will not be permitted to act on them. If you don't practice deceit, it will diminish. Therapy will help, too. This is also the time to renew your gym membership, start yoga, or at least take long walks. The victimization stuff must go.

## Forgiveness

Spike doesn't know it, but the biggest job he has left is learning how to forgive. You have learned that you need to wait for your child to take the lead. Lewis Smedes in his book *The Art of Forgiving* can help parents understand that their child has a challenge, too.

- In short, Spike's life will be compromised until he can forgive.
- The problem is he has no idea what forgiveness is or that he should somehow be expected to do it.
- Who does he need to forgive anyway?
- Until he figures that one out, the failure to forgive will prolong his tendency to take every step on the wrong foot and then be forced to remind himself about the right foot as he stumbles to self-correct.

Why not do it right the first time? Because it involves parents, not to mention an essentially naïve child.

What do you suppose it would take for Spike to forgive?

- He needs to understand that it is something he must do.
- He needs to understand what forgiveness is all about and why it matters. It takes time.
- Children do not readily forgive. It takes more wisdom and maturity than most children have.

A child's perspective is something like a tunnel. An adult perspective is more like a horizon. To get from tunnel to horizon takes experience in the world that usually only time can provide.

Therapy can probably help, but forgiveness is largely an adult phenomenon. Spike needs to struggle for a few years as he gains perspective. A child's perspective is something like a tunnel. An adult perspective is more like an horizon. To get from tunnel to horizon takes experience in the world that usually only time can provide.

Forgiveness is something we all have to do from time to time.

- Most of us must learn to forgive our parents for being human. Spike needs to do the same thing.
- We learn to put life's struggles in perspective and move on.
- A big part of forgiveness is giving up the need for vengeance, putting aside bitterness, and rationalizing disappointment.
- Spike needs to accept his parents as human and probably as humans who are no more or less frail than he is. It is a tall order.
- This does not mean that his parents were awful. Quite the contrary: it probably means that they were normal.

It means that children look to parents to keep them safe. Good intentions or not, not everyone can pull that off. When they don't, little Spikes emerge, and the little Spikes hold parents accountable.

Victims want justice. When it comes time to forgive, there is a difference between vengeance (which they must give up) and justice (which they don't need to give up).

- Just because you forgive whomever it was that stole the family jewels doesn't mean that the crook doesn't need to do the time. He does.
- If Spike feels a wrong requires justice, he can still give up vengeance.
- What would justice look like to Spike? That really depends on what he will accept.
- Hopefully it means he would accept parental love no matter how flawed or unavailable it was to him when he needed it most.
- He would, we hope, accept love with or without an apology.
- He would, we also hope, understand that the unhappiness he experienced was probably unwitting and unintentional.

> It means that children look to parents to keep them safe. Good intentions or not, not everyone can pull that off. When they don't, little Spikes emerge, and the little Spikes hold parents accountable.

If he waits for the whole loaf of life, that is to say parental perfection, he may never get it since none of us is perfect. Most of us come to accept parental imperfection as an unpleasant part of life and do just fine on a half a loaf. We supply the rest ourselves.

Why give up vengeance? Because vengeance won't feel good if it ever happens. We just think it will.

- We think that if the person who made us miserable could have a taste of what he did to us, then things could be all better. They won't.
- The bitterness will remain.
- The pain Spike suffered can't be duplicated in another.

The pain will always feel stronger in his heart than in the bleeding and broken body of his tormentor. He can't calibrate revenge so well that his pain and his tormenters pain feels exactly the same. They won't. Ever.

Forgiveness does not mean forgetting. Forgetting is basically impossible.

- It is too much to expect that we could somehow make hurt, especially the hurt that went on for the length of one's childhood, suddenly go away.
- One of the things that distinguishes us from many lower life forms is a complex memory.
- That means things that happen to us stay with us until they have no use, then we tend to assign them to a cobwebby corner of our mind.
- The process is liberating. It is like taking off a jacket that is too heavy.

The forgiver finds that he was hanging onto something that he didn't need. Memory of hurt exists forever but becomes inactive unless triggered. Memory stays; the hurtful impact of memory yields to inactivity and allows for goodness to happen.

Spike is having a disagreement. Spike has lots of disagreements.

# CHAPTER 5 : Frequently Asked Questions

**What is the typical Spike parent like?**
They often feel trapped, don't know what to do and turn to some combination of being angry, loud, threatening, critical, hypersensitive, frustrated, exhausted, and demanding.

**Will this program change my life?**
It's very likely, if you do it well.

**Can my book reading group do this together?**
No. P.A.C.T. is for the individual parent or at the most two parents

**What happens if my spouse refuses to participate?**
You do it by yourself. It will still work.

**Can single parents do this program?**
Yes, see above.

Counseling and P.A.C.T. attack two separate but overlapping parts of Spike's unhappiness: the long-term and the short-term. Training is short-term, not in the duration of its effects (which go on forever), but in the short time it takes to establish new habits. Short-term progress creates a vehicle that long-term can build upon.

**How will I know if it works?**
You'll know a lot in two months. Your growth or non-growth will be obvious.

**What's the most common complaint about P.A.C.T.?**
It's a tough program. The hard part is doing every step, one at a time

**What's the second most common complaint?**
"You mean I'm supposed to let the little S.O.B. get away with that?" Yes, temporarily. But don't worry; you'll get control.

**Third most common complaint?**
"You are telling me what not to do. Now tell me what TO do." It isn't necessary. P.A.C.T. trains behavior out, not in.

**If I teach myself P.A.C.T., will all my other children change too?**
Yes, but not all at the same rate.

**What is the difference between counseling and training?**
Counseling is the reverse of training. Training is time-limited, authoritarian, insistent on early success and goal-specific. It avoids insight, feelings and finding reasons for misery that are unnecessary to success in P.A.C.T. Its model is educational, not clinical or medical. It assumes that much of misery is learned and can be unlearned. P.A.C.T. encourages clients to become involved in counseling, if they are not already.

**Why don't you include children since they are part of the family too?**
If you include Spike in this program, he will destroy it. He is interested in staying in control. He will do so any way he can.

> We want Spike to give up the people, places, and things that maintain his awful behavior. But he won't do it. We have to do it for him. And, we have to do it through the back door. He has the front door barricaded by defensiveness, hypersensitivity, and threats.

**How do I use this book?**
There are two ways to use this book: as an accompaniment to training with the P.A.C.T. trainer or as a self-help guide.

**Who should use this book?**
Any parent, grandparent, aunt, or uncle who has care of an out-of-control child.

**What will be different about my child when the program is over?**
Rule of thumb: If you can count bad behavior—for instance, the number of times a week you are sworn at—it will stop. All bad behavior will moderate. It is a by-product of your changed approach to your child. You needn't count bad behavior to have it change. It will anyway. Counting a series of bad things your child does (or causes to happen) every week is a device. It allows you to see a connection between what you learn and your kid's change. More changes occur than are on the list. Some changes occur sooner, some later. Swearing at parents goes away before fighting between siblings; disrespect towards parents moderates before bad phone calls from school go away.

The bottom feeders

"Try and stop me!"

# CHAPTER 6 : Case Studies

## What are the Experiences of Other Families in P.A.C.T.?

The following are a series of vignettes of former participants in P.A.C.T. Names have been changed.

**Doris and Al:** A Daughter Who is an Outcast

Doris is a stay-at-home mom. Al, the husband and father, makes a comfortable professional salary and is often on the road. Their two girls—Rebecca and Jasmine, 14 and 12, respectively—have had a rough time as noted in the psychiatric labels and related behavior they both exhibit. The girls have been through it all: self-mutilation, mental hospital admissions, medication, and therapy. Their labels sort of helped because their parents could search the Internet and say, "Yup, that's our child!" but that didn't really change anything. Mom says that she only recently learned that her oldest daughter had been the victim of bullying several years ago but that the girl had kept it to herself out of shame.

The school apparently did not know any more than the parents. No one knew, except some of the children at school. The children used to pass around an "I Hate Rebecca Book" and write down all the reasons why everyone ought to hate Rebecca. They made sure Rebecca saw it. Apparently they did hate her, too, though it is difficult to understand the reason why. Probably nothing more than the simple cruelty of being outside the in-group in an upper middle class Connecticut neighborhood.

> The presumption that home would be a calm place meant that choices opened up to this family that they didn't know they would have.

But the experience was awful. It made for a child who was desperate to get away. Since her parents didn't understand, and Rebecca wouldn't reveal, they just staggered in the face of their daughter's intense anger and mood swings. The parents blamed themselves and so, they thought, did everyone else. Evidently her torturers grew tired of their play and moved on. But in the meanwhile, damage had been done. Then it was Jasmine's turn: a full-blown psychotic breakdown at school. These parents were almost beyond redemption. They were still together but only barely. Life with the girls had been hell. No one was on the same page, ever. No one could support the other, ever. But they proved to be wonderful, if initially skeptical, clients; the house did eventually settle down. The parents became the models of stability that these girls craved. They did it through the seemingly simple P.A.C.T. formula of exhibiting strength through patience. The need for acceptance of their daughter at her worst crept in, and however hellacious school was, home gradually became a sanctuary against a larger, non-accepting world. Due to Al's schedule, Doris was the client. She was able to fill him in on the assignments. Much to his credit, he did them. These parents had been reduced to a knot of generalized anger towards their children, the school, and life in general. Nothing had worked for the longest time. It was a relief to have P.A.C.T. constantly spare them the need to respond to anger. All anger did was torture them and have absolutely no positive effect on anyone else. Progress through the program was slow, but reports were good, so they plugged on week after week. In the end, they achieved a level of calmness they never believed possible. The presumption that home would be a calm place meant that choices opened up to this family that they didn't know they would have. The parents could go out by themselves to dinner occasionally without having to worry. The kids could go to the library, do what they needed to do, and come back without incident. Doris and Al sampled real life and loved it.

### Cindy: Fighting the School

Parents who have been through P.A.C.T. look at the world differently. They think the world is out of control. They notice how much of the world yells at children. They also notice that many of the yellers aren't just parents, but teachers and other human services professionals who should know better. Until they learn otherwise, they also assume that schools are experts in handling and understanding children. In fact, they are, if those children are normal. The abnormally developing child is at risk because schools vary so widely in how they handle them. Part of the risk is encountering the alleged professional who should be in a different line of work. The wealthier districts often seem to be the worst. They are interested in proving how many kids they can get into the Ivy Leagues; not in how many they can get into, say, residential treatment.

> Parents may be struggling against an unyielding bureaucracy, but it doesn't translate into making life easier.

Ms. Smith is a fourth-grade teacher. She is the teacher of Cindy's child, aged 9. Cindy worked her way through P.A.C.T. with little help from the school. Parents are encouraged to attempt a partnership with the school, but it doesn't always work. The school may or may not be interested. While Cindy was struggling with the challenge of learning self-control, she became aware that the teacher was loud and abusive. It was terrible to hear. For one thing, it reminded Cindy of how she used to sound which made her feel guilty. She wondered how any child could cope with such apparent rejection and still function. The answer was poorly.

Cindy attempted to speak with the teacher, to let her know about P.A.C.T. and how it had made such a difference in her life. The teacher was unimpressed. She gave the standard "I've got 25 other children" excuse and said yelling was the only way she could keep control. The irony of this tale is that Cindy had been an acquaintance of this teacher for quite some time, in and out of the school, yet it had never registered with her how awful the woman sounded. And yet there was nothing new about how the teacher communicated with children. Cindy got nowhere with the teacher and, in desperation, attempted to get the child's classroom changed. The principal gave her the standard, "I can't be changing teachers in mid-year; I can't be changing teachers just because some child doesn't get along; she is one of our best teachers. It must be something that your child is doing; tell her to try harder to get along." It is, at times, like this that parents begin to learn, official slogans aside, just exactly how child-centered the school really is.

This administrator type is well known to many P.A.C.T. parents. The road out of the swamp for children who are miserable is a hard one. These children are crude and get little sympathy, support, or encouragement. It is even worse when they can't count on their parents. Parents may be struggling against an unyielding bureaucracy, but it doesn't translate into making life easier. The children may come at their parents and say, "But, you weren't there for me," when in reality they were, although it didn't make any difference. A child expects his parents to protect him. Period. Schools can be both wonderful and horrible. It all seems very random.

## Suburbia: A Son Who is a Disappointment

A very upper middle class family in an exclusive town had a serious control problem with a son, Michael, age 17, a high school junior. This son had his own sports car. So did many of his comrades. Spending money was no problem. He got a hefty allowance. He was a low-average student. He'd make it into college, although hardly the college of Mom and Dad's dreams. It would probably be a state college which was not something that passed the lips of this outwardly polite family. Those colleges were for others. The matter of college was a problem. The child had heard about his family's long standing ties to a particular college practically from the moment of birth. They longed to maintain generational ties to this college. It was very important to these parents. Buildings had been named after family members, endowments established, and a substantial tradition followed. But it was not going to happen, even with a hefty donation to the endowment. The college had a legacy admissions program, but Junior was not going to make the cut.

> Life at home was not as pleasant. Hounding was the least of it. There was anger and plenty of it. The boy believed he was a disappointment and was reminded of such often. The family expected success.

The matter of college was, in fact, so important that the child had been hounded about grades for years. This year was no different. His parents tried everything they could: tutors, reward (the car), and punishments (loss of pocket money). Psychologists had been consulted. Maybe the child was depressed, they thought, so they tried psychiatrists, too. Nothing helped. He got himself to school. Not much happened after the bell rang. He didn't get into trouble at school and, in fact, seemed to enjoy being there. He just wasn't willing to put in any effort. He did absolutely no more than was required to stay eligible for sports. He seemed to know exactly what he could get away with and what he couldn't. Nobody ever said he wasn't bright.

Life at home was not as pleasant. Hounding was the least of it. There was anger and plenty of it. The boy believed he was a disappointment and was reminded of such often. The family expected success. This child became an embarrassment as friends asked, "I suppose Michael will go to_____this fall?" His parents stammered out a reply. Michael was not on the same track. Dad was impatient. He berated Michael for his lack of devotion to family. Mom just seemed sad.

Michael gradually responded by becoming angry, by breaking things, by swearing at his parents, by doing exactly what he wanted and nothing else. He was ruining his Dad's dream. "That's not all I can ruin," he once said.

It was a huge leap for this highly self-assured set of parents to engage P.A.C.T. Ordinarily, parents in this affluence level will attempt one more time to buy success, this time with some very expensive school somewhere. They could afford it. But something told them that it might only postpone problems that they would have to deal with sooner or later and might not work at all. Children run away from these kinds of places all the time. The position of P.A.C.T. has been to do the program well and then send him to the private school if he wants to go. He might actually benefit from the experience. Some of those schools can be wonderful, providing the kid hangs around to benefit. But to engage P.A.C.T. would be to change everything about how they interacted with the child and abandon every expectation they had as well. That led them to believe that if they wanted a relationship with their son, they had to get past grieving for the family tradition. They had to stop saying, "If only...."

> That led them to believe that if they wanted a relationship with their son, they had to get past grieving for the family tradition. They had to stop saying, "If only...."

These parents actually did quite well. They got their values straightened out. The child still went to a state college. He ended up being a special education teacher. Everyone turned out to be content. Everything that had once reminded them of their child's ability to stick a finger in the eye of their dreams had to pass unnoticed and unacknowledged. After a while, it got to be a habit. They found out that the long disappointment they thought their child was going to put them through was nothing of the kind.

### Martha and John: Young, Unstable, and Irritated

Martha and John produced a very unhappy first child. They were young. There wasn't much money. They moved a lot. They were distracted by trying to put their lives together. There was a lot of irritation between them.

There was occasional fighting. They weren't very supportive of one another and were very competitive. John wasn't particularly mature. He got into marriage as an escape from loneliness and failure. Martha got into marriage because that's what girls did. She genuinely liked John, at least at first.

Martha liked John because he wasn't her father. John liked Martha because she liked him. Before long, both began to feel disappointed in their mate, but they struggled on, somehow staying together. It wasn't a good mix, and it had its consequences. Should they divorce? They thought about it often, but somehow never got around to it. Neither wanted that kind of obvious failure. But a different kind of failure emerged: their son. By the time the boy was in middle school, he was pulling knives on his parents, staying out all night, taking drugs, and engaging in precocious sex. He responded to nothing. His favorite expression was, "Fuck you." Martha met verbal fire with verbal fire because she thought that she could control the child through yelling, anger, criticism, sarcasm, and all the rest. John, who was a detached father anyway, at least used the detachment to the ultimate advantage of his son by learning this program. Martha did not.

Martha allowed herself the luxury of denial of this child's problems and the surprises that often happened because of it. Since she was always surprised at the stunts the child pulled, she never had a decent strategy to overcome them. He could manipulate her into a reaction with great skill. Sometimes it was hard to figure out whether she was really as naïve as she seemed or just couldn't bear the thought of her child's problems. Years later, he still has his problems, but he has made lots of progress. He graduated from college. He holds down a job. He can be just as successful as he wants to be. But dealing with him requires a thorough understanding of codependence and the clear boundaries that rejecting codependence requires. One of the parents has that understanding, the other does not. So the competition continues. The son would be in better shape if both did. Parenting never stops. Trying to get parents to be partners evidently doesn't stop, either.

> Sometimes it was hard to figure out whether she was really as naïve as she seemed or just couldn't bear the thought of her child's problems.

## Sarah: She's Married, But She's Still a Single Parent

Sarah has a part-time husband. That is, Bill is a husband and father, but he isn't around much and when he is, he's grouchy. Actually, he is more than grouchy; he swears constantly. Every word is "F… this" and "F… that." It gets tiresome and certainly doesn't help anything. It's also just the tip of Bill's iceberg. Underneath the swearing is a discontented man. Sarah has the responsibility for their pregnant teenage daughter almost exclusively on her shoulders. Bill doesn't want any part of it, saying, "She did it. She can live with it."

Bill's disappointment in his daughter isn't anything particularly unusual; his dreams for her went up in smoke. Of course, Bill doesn't understand that his dyspeptic view on life may have contributed indirectly to all of this failure. This girl's pregnancy was the natural consequence of a long-term suicidal depression. How she became involved with her hapless boyfriend is anyone's guess. But soon enough they were planning how wonderful life would be when they collectively moved away from their parents and set up their nest. It didn't work out that way. It wasn't long after the birth that the new mommy and daddy were no longer on speaking terms. And grandpa was off in some corner cursing about how tough life was.

So Sarah had not only her daughter's depression to deal with, she also had a dysfunctional husband, a new grandchild, and a child-father to cope with. The detachment, which she learned from P.A.C.T., and the selective reattachment meant that she was able to negotiate uncharted waters with increasing confidence most days. It was a relief to no longer be sucked into everyone's problems. Their problems were their problems. It turns out that knowing who you are and knowing where you stand is a wonderful insulation from others who have yet to organize their own lives. Instead of leaving the parental home the minute she turned sixteen, the new mother returned to high school. In fact, all things considered, this was a pretty happy conclusion. The future was far from decided, but at least it didn't look as grim as it used to. Sarah ended up doing a lot of changing, and so did her daughter. Sarah, of course, didn't want to raise a second family, but the options were grim, so she did.

Aside from the new father, who essentially dropped out of the picture, the one who made some of the most sought after change was Sarah's husband, who had refused to participate not merely in P.A.C.T. but in much of anything else. Her efforts at P.A.C.T. generalized as it normally does. If clients focus just on their kid, they just get kid change. If they focus on the world, all kinds of changes occur. While Sarah's husband was never much of a prize, he seemed to relax better than anyone had imagined. Over time, he moderated his grouchiness, took some interest in the baby, and participated in his daughter's life. He was no longer the weight that seemed to drag everyone backward.

### Jane: Barely Concealed Hatred for a Son

Jane, a registered nurse, has a son who is not the apple of her eye. In fact, she may have even hated the boy. She would never admit it. She couldn't stand the guilt. But her behavior, verbal and otherwise, gave her away. One thing very clear about Jane is that she is terribly confused. You might be confused too if you led a difficult life, and one of the reinforcers of that life was a child of yours who came to you via a violent rape. She didn't believe in abortion, so she delivered the child. She has been angry ever since. The boy sets the agenda for the home. He steals. He lies. He gets in trouble at school and in the neighborhood. The police come and go. He refers to her in her face as "Bitch" as in, "Hey, Bitch, bring me…."

Jane hasn't a shred of motherly influence over him and she is too consistently angry to learn any. Jane struggles against herself continually, but you can tell in her voice just how she feels. Tone of voice is a dead give-away. She makes all kind of pronouncements and follows through on none of them. She booby-traps every good thing he does, and he responds with violence. She complains about him without end. Thus, the boy went to a foster placement and will be there permanently. This is a good plan. But it isn't the end of the story. It is an unusual conclusion for P.A.C.T., however.

Jane can visit the boy, and the boy can visit her. She didn't initially want to do that because to be rid of him was to be rid of her attacker. They can learn to have a relationship, but it is unlikely that they can live together. She will need to return to court and have the order reversed for that to happen, and it probably won't happen. She is unlikely to take that step.

> You might be confused too if you led a difficult life, and one of the reinforcers of that life was a child of yours who came to you via a violent rape.

For Jane, attempting to learn how to manage her child partially succeeded and partially didn't, at least in the short term. With the child out of the home, she was able to concentrate on learning what she needed to learn in P.A.C.T. and was able to practice it during visits. The visits gradually become much better and longer. She took him for the day. She occasionally brought him home for a sleep-over. His behavior was terrific, and so was hers. She was actually taking pleasure in him and looked forward to visits. Yet she knew that if he returned to her home it would start up all over again. She concluded he was better off where he was with frequent visits from her. Maybe she was right. She did learn, almost by accident, that she had more feeling for the boy than she thought possible. It took—and continues to take—some distance for her to see it.

These two have a long way to go before they can be permanently in one another's company. It may, in fact, never happen and maybe it shouldn't. The pressure of not living together is a whole lot less. They both do much better apart with frequent visits than they did together. It happened because, with some distance, she was able to learn how to avoid his traps for her. Once that began to happen, she felt a different kind of freedom, not merely the freedom that came with the separation. She learned she was not obligated to respond to his baiting and as she didn't, he ceased. She also did something that she swore she'd never do: went to counseling. She always assumed that counseling was silly because all you did was sit around and talk about your problems which is, of course, true.

## Barbara: A Single Mom Who Fell Apart, But Pulled Herself Back Together Again

After Barbara was divorced, she fell apart. She had led a comfortable life previously but she didn't have an education so there was little she had to rely on when she was on her own. Barbara had a very hard time supporting herself and her daughter. Every day was a struggle.

One night at a party a friend introduced her to cocaine which she grew to crave. Since she couldn't afford it she dabbled in the call girl business. That lead to a pregnancy. She got into P.A.C.T. through a referral by the state which was threatening to take her daughter. Her daughter didn't have the best opportunity to grow normally with the divorce and her mother falling apart. When Barbara would pull herself together, she'd sit her daughter down and give her a lecture about life. Barbara was not in a good position to be lecturing anyone, and it wasn't long before that these lessons in "how-to-lead-your-life-differently-than-I-led-mine" got really old.

> Of course, it wasn't just the lecturing; it was the drug-induced unavailability of her mother and the really lousy parenting that happened whether she was sober or not that made the biggest difference.

Lecturing was about the only thing that Barbara had to offer. The preaching began to have the opposite effect than Barbara wanted. In spite of what her mom said, or maybe because of it, the child was rapidly getting out of control. Of course, it wasn't just the lecturing; it was the drug-induced unavailability of her mother and the really lousy parenting that happened whether she was sober or not that made the biggest difference. By the time of the referral, Barbara was married to a guy, Abe, who knew her background but didn't seem to care. She had recently gotten herself off drugs and attended NA meetings probably due to pressure from the state. Abe seemed to love her which was a stroke of good fortune for her. They had two additional children and settled down to a conventional, although financially marginal, life. Interestingly enough, her daughter accepted Abe, which was good for everyone. It doesn't usually work that way.

But there were more challenges to come. Barbara had an intermittent problem with anger, which led her into explosive hitting sessions when one of the youngsters didn't do what she thought he should do. One of her boys told his teacher. The teacher told the principal, and the principal called the state. Both Barbara and Abe were upset that the state was in their life. In an unusual turnabout, they were able to put aside their anger and concentrate on their lives. They became model clients and produced one of the most unusual changes of any family. The changes seemed too good to be true, and the state kept the case open even longer than normal in such situations. Eventually, even the state became convinced that these parents were genuine. The turnaround for Barbara was an illustration of how even the most unpromising circumstances can yield to change when parents want it badly enough.

### Gene and Mary: A Very Disturbed Daughter

Gene and Mary lived the quiet suburban life. Well, to call it quiet is stretching things a bit because their teenage daughter, age 15, was anything but quiet. She had recently been released from a psychiatric hospital. That may conjure up pictures of bona fide nuttiness, but psychiatric hospitals are commonly used for children who can't control themselves and are at some serious risk of harm to themselves or others. In fact, in most states, if a child is brought into an emergency room because that child, say, threatened suicide, the emergency room is legally required to find a bed in a psychiatric hospital for that child. Moreover, that child can't legally be released from the emergency room until that happens. Once found, children are brought in, kept for a number of days, and released when they are found to have been "stabilized." Stabilization is a situation imposed by insurance companies that do not want to pay for hospitalizations, which then don't normally last more than a week anyway.

> The parents refused to accept that their daughter's intermittent explosive rages or the stealing might be an expression of victimization.

Anyway, it was determined much later, that this teenage daughter was a probable incest victim when she was small. Prior to this determination, she had been the target of many accusations due to her behavior. If something disappeared, she took it. If something bad happened, she was in the middle of it. If family plans got spoiled, they would look no further than her. There is nothing she wasn't accused of. There was reason, of course, as she continually stole things belonging to family members. After all, something important was stolen from her, she was just trying to even the score. The fact that the score can never be evened is something the girl has yet to learn.

The perpetrator? Probably her brother. He still lived at home, seemed like a nice enough kid and was about to finish high school when this program began. The parents refused to accept that their daughter's intermittent explosive rages or the stealing might be an expression of victimization. They just thought she was bad. There was no proof. The brother certainly wasn't talking. The girl returned home from her "stabilization" to an unchanged setting. Some anger can outlast most anything tossed at it. The parents were told that even if the stabilization didn't faze the daughter, they might learn calmness in the face of her rage. In addition to the various counseling and other services, the family was referred to P.A.C.T.

Interestingly enough, the family did well. They initiated the program about as skeptically as anyone else but were so desperate that they knocked themselves out to do it. And it worked. The alleged sexual abuse is something that will have to be worked out one way or another in the family; after all, it is still just an allegation. But it is clear that the family functions in a much calmer manner due to P.A.C.T. The daughter has responded nicely as well. She seems to have given up her rage, rejoined the family, gained an interest in school, and generally seems headed in the right direction. This isn't the same thing as a cure, but it may have set the scene for eventual healing. She and the rest of the family wisely go to therapy. Perhaps a combination of therapy and calmness will produce a resolution.

### An Anonymous Couple: Dad Arrested

When an adolescent girl stays away from home for days at a time, the initial question is what is wrong with the child? Often that is the wrong question. The right question is: what is this child running from? It is not always obvious.

P.A.C.T. was sent to a middle class home in the suburbs. Both parents were engaged in professional careers. They had two children. One, 16, seemed to be content. The other, 17, was in terrible shape. From the curb, there was one clue as to the problem: all the shades were drawn.

> The family had suffered a great deal of turmoil in the past with Dad, and now with his absence it struggled to settle into some semblance of a normal household. Mom emerged as a strong, reliable figure.

This often suggests that the occupants have removed themselves from the world at some level. It is often a signal of depression. In the front parlor, the problem was not obvious. The house looked lived in, but not terrible. P.A.C.T. spends little time trying to understand problems. It is interested in whether or not parents can do P.A.C.T. If they say they can, they start work. P.A.C.T. is not immune, however, from spotting clues.

The next clue came in conversation with the parents. These parents seemed quite interested in the program, but they complained about everything; the school, their parents, the neighborhood, their therapist, etc. They had little grasp of their situation, but what they did acknowledge was that what happened was someone else's fault. Sometimes, first sessions are awkward as new clients aren't quite sure how to act. But this came across as more than first session nervousness. They plowed on ahead.

Attendance was never an issue nor was compliance with the goals. They seemed to neither go too fast through the program nor too slowly. Some goals were tough and required more time. Both seemed equally engaged. Communication between the two seemed good. They cued one another. The household calmed down. Things were going very well when all of a sudden the daughter ran away from home again.

All participants in P.A.C.T. are told that midway through the program, just as things are calming down, the difficult child will pull some kind of stunt. It happens so commonly that P.A.C.T. assumes the child is testing the determination of parents. Parents who are not taken by surprise and manage the test well, do fine; the problem recedes. At these times, the child tends to re-work old parental vulnerabilities.

Parents who don't do well with the mid-term test give their child a signal that parents can, in fact, be successfully beaten. This is not a good signal. The problem with this family did not immediately recede. The program continued. Two or three weeks passed, and the daughter had not returned. Dad was not available for an appointment either, just Mom. This was a first. Dad, it turned out, had been arrested.

It was revealed that Dad was a long-term alcoholic whose enrollment in P.A.C.T. was a court-ordered condition of remaining in the home. This was unknown to P.A.C.T., but it didn't need to be known either. Knowing wouldn't have changed anything. Ordinarily court orders to P.A.C.T. fail unless the parent has first taken the time to understand P.A.C.T. and, second, wants it. Dad was highly motivated so the order from the bench seemed to work except he got drunk one night, apparently for the first time since the program started. His daughter, who was still in the home at the time, made a sarcastic remark to him. He hit her. She told her mother. Mom called the police. Dad was arrested. Daughter ran off.

The child did not return until it was clear that Dad would not be permitted back in the home. Things got serious for Dad as he was soon fired from his job. Mom filed for divorce. She also continued with the program and did well. It concluded successfully and without incident. The family had suffered a great deal of turmoil in the past with Dad, and now with his absence it struggled to settle into some semblance of a normal household. Mom emerged as a strong, reliable figure.

As stories go, this family worked at one level. The girl returned home and stayed there. Mom did a great job of keeping her family, minus the husband, together and functioning. At another level, the tragedy of alcoholism claimed another family which was left to cope with its destruction. The coping will go on for years. The kids will long for an absent father, but will be reluctant to spend much time around him. As it happens, the reluctance will be a court-ordered restriction on his contact with them. He is unable to do so without a monitor.

### Helen and Carl: A Controller Keeps a Child Unbalanced

Helen lived with Carl and her two children, aged 8 and 9, on the top floor of a walk-up apartment house. Money was a problem, but the place was always neat. Carl worked, but, because of her son, Helen did not. Her son had been diagnosed with Asperger's Syndrome, an autism subtype characterized by frequent rages and a poor ability to interact with others. Helen and Carl had lived together quite a while, and the children seemed attached to him. That did not prevent Carl from raging right back at the boy. He did not accept, nor did he try to accommodate, the boy's disability. The household was in chaos. The school often called Helen, telling her how awful the day was for the boy. Ultimately, a day treatment program was found for the boy.

*Parents who complete the program know when they are slipping and what the costs of those slips are.*

When P.A.C.T. was initiated, Helen and Carl participated together. It took just a few short weeks to figure out that Carl had no intention of learning to control himself. Indeed, that turned out to be a big part of the problem. Carl was a controlling personality, and controllers are loath to give up control, whether they are adults or children. The Basic Goal portion of the program needed to be lengthened, but it was done only with the understanding that Carl could not participate. He had smiled and seemed cooperative during the sessions, but behind the scenes he undercut progress. Helen cried often, and they even split up for a week or so over the way he treated her. But she wanted to keep on going so she did, alone. For her part, it was soon revealed that Helen had some substantial problems with depression and that her relationship with Carl was a desperate attempt to find someone who could lead her through life because she didn't have the courage to do so herself. One of the ways that her depression asserted itself was through her need to talk incessantly. Constantly. On and on. The talk seemed to go nowhere or result in change. Her talking was widely ignored in the family or used as an excuse for great exasperation by everyone. P.A.C.T. gradually compelled her to focus. P.A.C.T. can't compel anything that its clients don't want. Helen wanted to learn.

Without Carl, progress was rapid. There were the occasional stumbles, and the boy had bad days from time to time, but the number and severity of his rages declined almost to nothing. Helen gradually felt a sense of accomplishment. School was going well for the boy. Home life was peaceful. Carl seemed to be cooperating from a distance. The service concluded with wishes for continued happiness all around. Word filtered back later, however, that Carl reasserted himself now that Helen's supports were gone and, within weeks, the household completely reverted back to its former self. Months later word filtered back again: Helen and Carl were arrested for physical abuse, and the child was removed by the state. She was quoted as saying she knew she had violated every rule in P.A.C.T., but that since she knew what to do once, she could figure it out again. Parents who complete the program know when they are slipping and what the costs of those slips are. But Helen was an emotionally thin reed who chose someone to support her who couldn't and wouldn't.

Helen was ultimately as good as her word, however. She found the strength to cut Carl out of her life. It was an act of bravery on her part. She had never been without a partner who didn't take the dominant role in her life. The court restored her son to her, and while life was a challenge, she seemed to soldier on well enough. She did not let Carl return and as long as she is able to find this strength, she will do fine.

### Dan: A Single Dad in Recovery

Dan is in recovery from alcoholism. He attends AA several times a week. He works full time and has either two or three children living with him, depending on the day and their disposition.

One of the children, a son age 12, wanders around the neighborhood day and night, and Dan often isn't entirely sure where the boy is. His marriage to an alcoholic fell apart shortly after Dan became sober. Dan was awarded custody and he lives in a converted garage. Just because Dan was awarded custody does not mean that he was a particularly good parent. But he was better than his wife. He is learning quickly.

P.A.C.T. seemed to strengthen his sobriety because of the calmness he was able to produce. Although he was always worried about his son wandering the streets, it happened that, bit by bit, the boy started coming around home. First it was just for a quick pop-in, then a longer visit. Then a meal. Then he crashed on the couch and stayed the night. Dan had left the boy's room just the way the boy had left it when he split,

> He learned to wait for the child to get comfortable and offer up information on his own terms and in his own time. He was rewarded by his son's permanent return.

so it wasn't hard for the boy to fit back in. Dan learned how to detach himself, how to accept the boy at the boy's own level and how to have faith that things would probably turn out all right if he completely changed how he interacted with the boy. Part of the strategy was his decision not to question his son on where he was, who he was with, or how he was getting along. When the child showed up at the apartment, Dan just said, "Hi," and let his son take it from there. If it was near mealtime, which it almost always was, Dan just said, "I'm cooking dinner," and he made extra which generally went into his son. He learned to wait for the child to get comfortable and offer up information on his own terms and in his own time. He was rewarded by his son's permanent return. If this begins to look like a technique to get a deer to lick salt from your hand, you are right. The deer is afraid and will bolt in an instant. Your role is just to be there with the salt cube for however long it takes for the deer to relax his fear. If you take the occasion to seem threatening, you'll never see that deer again. Acceptance of a problem child follows the same principal. Dan was clearly a parent, but his options in parenting were limited if he wanted this to work. He did. The son settled in well. The settling was tentative at first, but, subsequently was comfortable.

### Jan: A Single Mom With a Psychotic Ex-husband

Jan felt she was losing her grip. She was a single mom with a psychotic ex-husband and a vulnerable child, aged 16, who had been brutalized by the divorce and by his now-absent father. The child was on his way to a residential placement. Jan really didn't want it. She couldn't see how it would help. But she was desperate. She knew what she was doing was not working. She saw no alternative. She thought it was a risk that she thought she probably had to take. She understood that the state can't be a surrogate parent no matter how optimistic they promote the possibility of voluntary removal.

The father was still in the picture and often told his son, "Be ready Friday at 5," and then never showed up. The father also showed no remorse. Instead, he found something about the boy to pick on. He did it repeatedly. Intentionally or not, the father wanted to give the boy the impression that waiting on the curb for a father that rarely came, was the boy's fault. It worked. Naturally, the boy thought the way he was treated had something to do with him. After all, no decent kid would be treated this way by a parent. What was the matter with him? What was he doing that was so awful? He redoubled his efforts at being a good boy. He was promptly at the curb waiting, and waiting. The child took out his sadness and his resentment on his mother. Maybe it was her fault too, he thought. His dad might say that something else more important came up or might not say anything. It is no wonder that the boy coped with this mess through depression, which was formally diagnosed as bipolar disorder. He also developed a compulsion for lining up shoes although his room looked like the town dump. Mom went to therapy. The boy refused.

The child's mood swings were frequent and wide. He raged and threw things at his mother and anyone else within range. Whenever he became upset, he went for his shoes and lined them up on his hands and knees with a ruler. Then he did the same thing with his toys. He'd become upset at anything. Even a perturbed look on his mother's face could send him rocketing out of control. It is also no wonder that the ex-husband blamed his former wife for the child's condition. Jan was in surprisingly good shape emotionally and committed relatively few of the errors presented in P.A.C.T.

However, it was decided that if this program was to be successful, even a single violation of any of the goals was too much for this highly sensitive child. She committed herself to the awareness that this program requires and demonstrated that mood swings and compulsions can be controlled. The symptoms all but disappeared because Mom learned to present herself as the essence of calm, predictability, and strength, all without a hint of the frustration that is interpreted as criticism and rejection. The child developed the ability to communicate with his mother. School improved. Medications were eliminated. And all conversation about finding this child a residential placement ceased.

This does not suggest that the child will not continue to have adjustment problems, because he will. But it does show that a home life which can be made to be relatively pressure free can go a long way to creating a willingness to risk school success and social success. And as for the shoes? The line-up yielded a permanent pile in the middle of the room.

**Linda:** Newly Separated From a Non-Communicative and Non-Participating Husband

After 20 years, Linda said that she had given up. The last 10 years were just for the children, she said. Linda's husband wasn't a bad parent, just uncommunicative. When there were problems, he crawled into his shell and left Linda to cope. She was tired of being on the firing line all alone. He probably thought he was being strong. In fact, he was escaping. Now that the oldest boy, Bill 15, was arrested and briefly sent to detention, Linda thought enough was enough. She told John to leave.

> When there were problems, he crawled into his shell and left Linda to cope. She was tired of being on the firing line all alone.

The program started before the couple split, and John, true to form, was indifferent to both the program and the need for the program. Indifference just gave Linda added incentive to insist on a split. In fact, she used the program to cope as much with her now ex-husband as she did with the children left at home. And she did very well. The oldest boy was released but not to his mother; Linda refused to have him. She wasn't ready yet, she said and she didn't think the child was ready either. John stepped up to take the boy, which was either courageous or foolish depending on perspective. He still would not participate in the program

Swapping households didn't work, of course. These arrangements almost never do. The child was back with Mom in two weeks. The child wouldn't do as he was told. The child was disrespectful. John said either do it my way or you are history. So, the child was history. And John? As far as he was concerned, he'd done his best and was entirely justified in cutting off contact. Bill wasn't back in the maternal home for long before he started up with his mom. She initially fell back on her tried and true parenting, the kind that helped get her in the hole she was in now. Her enrollment in P.A.C.T. gave her a rapid about-face. It took Bill a while to realize he couldn't manipulate his mom. It took Mom a while to realize that things such as reminding him how awful he was in the past, how his behavior had resulted in a residential placement, and how he had few decent friends due to his lousy past characterized her parenting. She dropped it quickly upon learning.

Bill's dad resumed limited contact which was better than nothing. Bill stayed where he was and ended up doing fine.

### Gordon and Deb: Moved as Far Away as They Could Get

Gordon and Deb had been through a great deal. There was a serious upset in Gordon's family. After he had devoted many years to the family business, the rug was pulled out from under him by another faction of the family. So Gordon and Deb moved as far away in the same state as physically possible and cut off most contact. The bitterness of the experience took a while to get past. Gordon bought an inexpensive franchise and started his own business. It took a lot of time and effort to make it work. Gordon's parents came to see them once a year but those visits were strained. Gordon held his father responsible for all that had gone wrong. He was a long way from feeling forgiving. Those trips brought all of his resentment to the surface, and he was not a nice person to be around.

On top of that, Gordon and Deb's oldest daughter, now in middle school, was struggling, probably as a function of all the anger. The tension, anger, and disappointment in the household had been too much for her. She turned to drugs, early sex, and a collection of bottom of the barrel friends. School was a distant memory. Her behavior escalated into rages. She broke furniture, assaulted other siblings and finally got placed in a mental hospital. She just stayed a few days. She was discharged to home. She refused to attend special schools and always got herself thrown out if she was forced. The walls of their house were peppered with holes where she had banged her fist through them. They had been in every program imaginable. It took a while for them to calm down and, work the steps successfully, but, as they did they were astounded to see a correlation in their daughters behavior. In time, Gordon and Deb became poster children for P.A.C.T. Several years later, the daughter got her GED, held down a full time job, and maintained her own apartment. Her folks did not help her out with expenses. She visits frequently. One of the hardest things they had to do was put their bitterness about the larger family and the negativity that went with it aside. Forcing themselves to be positive when they felt like nothing of the kind was good exercise because it gradually turned into real feelings of anticipation, not phony wooden ones. Though it is true that we can't be something we aren't, practicing something different can lead to change.

> Forcing themselves to be positive when they felt like nothing of the kind was good exercise because it gradually turned into real feelings of anticipation, not phony wooden ones.

### Reverend Smith: A Rebellious Daughter

Reverend Smith had struggles blending his theology with his child, a girl aged 13. He was unsure about what he needed, where he should search, or what he should expect to find. He studied the scriptures for guidance. He didn't make progress. He thought that maybe the stain of original sin had produced all of his family unhappiness and that it was futile to try to make a difference. Maybe he should just accept that the daughter was the way she was by design and that it would be presumptuous of him to try to make it otherwise. Maybe pain and misery were part of the plan. Maybe it was a test of some sort. P.A.C.T. told him that only he could resolve those issues. He was encouraged to take the "acceptance" part seriously, but only because it would likely produce the best outcome. He had to decide whether having the courts and Child Protection in his life was something he needed to struggle against.

It is tempting to look at an unhappy child and conclude, as did the minister, that some children are born evil. P.A.C.T. hears variants of this all the time. Behavior seems so awful, so extreme, and so constant that this sort of conclusion is almost inevitable. But that doesn't make it correct. His daughter was a mess: truant, promiscuous, utterly disrespectful, and a thief. She didn't help the man's standing among his flock. But then she didn't want to, either. She called him a hypocrite and a liar not because he necessarily was, but because it sounded mean. In fact, some children do differ in their genetic inheritance which may make them vulnerable, under certain circumstances, to behavior that may makes them seem evil. It is the position of P.A.C.T. that this fact is either not permanent or else it is at least malleable.

> It is tempting to look at an unhappy child and conclude, as did the minister, that some children are born evil.

But Reverend Smith decided that he would not give in to the presumption of her apparent natural evilness; he would try to do what he could to change it. Once past his initial dilemmas, he did well. For one thing, his impulse to get the girl to talk to him was abandoned. It was clear she would not do it, and all his attempts had failed. His ministerial imperative to offer comfort and solace were met with unveiled contempt:

"Who the hell are you to be telling me what to do?" she scolded. "I hate you."

The "hate" part hurt, but he had to accept it. Hatred was the reverse of everything the man stood for, so it was a double assault, and his daughter knew it. But he could draw on another tradition—tolerance, forbearance, and patience, which he learned very well. The daughter did what most daughters do in the face of unalloyed acceptance—calmed down. He concluded the program exceptionally satisfied because he was able to blend both theology and his own impulse to make things better.

# PART II
## Parenting Spike

# How To Use The Charts

In the Appendix are a series of charts. Four of them are for keeping track of parent goals. Four of them are for parents to keep track of their kid's reactions as parents learn those goals. We will call them "Parent Charts" and "Child Charts" even though both are maintained by parents

Since it is may take a year to get through the program, we have thoughtfully divided the year into 4 segments of 13 weeks each. When you have completed the first segment of 13, go on to the next. Same with the Child Charts.

Each week you track your behavior. Each week you track how your child is reacting. So, both Parent and Child Charts should be the same. For instance, week 12 on one chart should be week 12 on the other chart.

**Parent chart:** Each week you will introduce yourself to a new goal, but only if you earned it. The goals appear in order. If you committed **four or fewer errors** on each weeks goal, you may select the next goal in line. Hold yourself to the highest possible standard. If you think something may be, oh, say, sarcasm, then mark it as sarcasm.

**Remember:** making errors to anyone in the universe counts against you. You are practicing on everyone, including your hideous mother-in-law, that worthless ex of yours or the nasty type-A jerk who cuts you off in traffic. Giving the jerk a one-fingered salute counts against you. Mouthing "You sonofabitch!" to him or her without actually saying it, also counts against you. Got the idea?

The last box in each week is the space where you write in the total. Make 5 errors this week? Then you stay put. Either work on the area that you had the problem, or concentrate on Goal Three: "Distract Yourself."

**Child Chart:** There are eight (8) target behaviors you want to disappear. So each week you write in the number of times any of those 8 occurred to YOU, not to the neighbors, not to other kids in the house, but YOU (or you and your partner, if both of you are working P.A.C.T. together.) You can add other specific target behaviors to the list that you want to see disappear. They probably will. Normally, this list is sufficient for most parents.

# CHAPTER 7 : The Three Basic Goals

# Basic Goal #1 : "Shh-h-h!"

## What's the Goal?

**No Yelling.** You will learn to speak so quietly that you can't be heard in the next room.

## What's in the Fine Print?

**Yelling is obvious.** We all know it when we hear it. But some may say that yelling is a matter of opinion, as in: "I was just emphasizing," or, "I was just raising my voice so you could hear me," or, "I just have a naturally loud voice."

The last one is a favorite. That is to say, if it is natural, then it is out of my control and everyone has to live with it. All these rationalizations must go. Otherwise, problems with your Spike will magnify.

Every parent is skeptical, initially, about trying to thread themselves through the eye of the P.A.C.T. needle in an effort to transform their child. For one, they get stuck at yelling and confuse it with virtue. It doesn't work. P.A.C.T. looks for the parent who is willing to put this and other reasons aside and get to work.

- **Many parents yell at their children all the time.** When parents are told to stop they often notice that: (1) they yell more than they thought they did; (2) everyone ignores them anyway; and (3) the only thing they get out of the bargain is exhaustion.
- **Parents do not get the very thing they want most out of yelling: compliance.** Parents who yell get more resistance, noncompliance, and anger. There are two times in a child's life when our Spike is most apt to be physically abused: when young and easily overpowered and when a young adolescent, because he is growing and threatens resistance. Think it can't happen to you and your Spike? Think again. You know better than anyone your occasional temptation to wring his neck.
- **Yelling may get worse over time; it takes more volume to get the same poor results.** Yelling is not punishment. It isn't perceived as punishment. Punishments that don't punish, reward. They enable non-compliance.

- **A parent's mouth is a poor weapon.** All they shoot are blanks. The words that come out are apt to be: (1) mean things that parents can't back up; (2) mean things that make matters worse; and (3) mean things that children ignore. If a mouth is only a weapon to be ignored, it is not much of a weapon.
- **Spike knows you are shooting blanks.** To make matters worse, he manipulates you into shooting them. All the while, you think you are actually in control. Spike knows differently. He is in control, and he knows it.
- **Yelling is yelling.** There is no distinction between good yelling and bad yelling. It is all yelling. Yelling in anger or in convenience is all the same. Yelling up the stairs is yelling. Yelling out the back door is yelling.

Remember: You are trying to convince yourself that you never need to raise your voice unless a serious, bona fide safety issue occurs. To make this easy, your goal is that you are so soft-spoken you can't be heard from room to room. So, answer the question of the week: How many times could you be heard from room to room?

## What's the Last Word?

Living with a tough child is tough. You have a lot of resentment and some days you could easily throttle him. Some days you don't feel the least bit loving. But try to do the following in some combination every day: Look your child in the eye, smile, give a gentle touch, and say something pleasant. And, unlovable though they may be, see if you can tell them once a week that you do, in fact, love them. If you can't do this and/or if you child can't handle it, don't worry about it. Time is on your side.

## What Did I Accomplish This Week?

This is the fun part. You pretend you are back in school. The better your homework, the better the results. Keep track of your and/or your spouse's daily progress in the space provided at the end of this goal. Prove to yourself what a good student you are in three steps:

1. Keep track of your progress using the scoring chart that follows each goal.
2. Keep track of your child's behavior on the same scoring chart.
3. Keep track of both parent and child behavior on the graph at the end of the book.

Count both parents if both are participating. If the child hears yelling from both, then both are contributing to this child's total pressure level. Otherwise, just do one. You may decide that you want to track just one child's errors or do all the children. Whatever your choice, be consistent. Don't change in midstream.

Remember The Four Error Rule: Your weekly goal is four errors. You may not yell more than four times in any seven-day period. If your spouse participates, neither of you may yell more than four times total in the week. If you can honestly say that you have not yelled (i.e., were not heard from room to room) then you can go onto the next goal. If not, stick with "No Yelling" until you have mastered it. Keep your standards high. The higher your standards, the better the outcome.

# Basic Goal #2 : What? Me? Angry?

## What's the Goal?

Don't display anger.

## What's in the Fine Print?

**Anger is a good thing in some settings.** P.A.C.T. will teach Spike's parents to show him how anger is most effectively used. It teaches through modeling. In short, anger to be effective needs to be rare, appropriate and controlled.

- **There is an implied contract in any emotion, including anger (i.e., I'll smile if you will smile back).** Anger used badly prompts the same implied contract.
- **Parents insist** that, "I can get angry at you, but that does not mean that you can get angry back at me again." Don't kid yourself.
- **A major short-term goal in P.A.C.T. is to stop all anger display.** A long-term goal is to display anger effectively. This means that for the time being, parents are not permitted to display or express anger to anyone or anything. We want our anger to seem virtuous so that our neighbors will say, "I don't know how you do it with that child!! How you must suffer, you poor dear. 'Course if it was up to me, I'd chloroform the little snake, but you are a better person than I am."
- **The presence of anger may not have originated with a child, but children are wonderfully able to encourage it.** No one can mandate the elimination of child-directed anger. You either can eliminate it or you can't. Those who can

The biggest mountain parents climb before they are successful in P.A.C.T. is acceptance of their role in anger. This does not mean that Spike's problem is or isn't a parent-created problem. It means that parents must make some basic sacrifices in order to see their pivotal role in this miserable child's life. Giving up anger is one of those sacrifices.

are in a much better position to do something substantial for their child. Those who can't need to see a therapist.

- **Eliminating anger is a tough goal.** Parents who are able to complete this goal discover that the anger they normally displayed was pointless
- **A little anger goes a long way.** Some parents regard anger as the most important of all emotions. Some parents congratulate themselves for having high standards, but without a child who follows them, the standards are meaningless.
- **When anger becomes excessive, someone needs to call a halt.** In fact, any display of anger is probably too much for an emotionally disturbed child to tolerate.
- **Anger is useful if it gets someone what they want.** What they ought to want is respect, appropriate control and happiness. They don't happen in a vacuum. They won't happen in the presence of anger.
- **P.A.C.T. depends on parental willingness and ability to change a large variety of destructive habits of which anger is frequently at the center.** Anger is frequently the defining characteristic of the unhappy family. Removing anger may radically change the family atmosphere and the dynamics

> There is a difference between anger and desperation. Anger is the emotion and desperation the result. The P.A.C.T. parent has both. Everything has been tried. Nothing works. Hopelessness rears its head. But desperation can be useful. While it makes some parents give up, it makes others receptive. P.A.C.T. looks for the latter.

**What's the Last Word?**

Living with a tough child is tough, but everyday, try to do the following in some combination: Look your child in the eye, smile often, give a gentle touch, and say something pleasant. And unloving though they may be, see if you can tell them once a week that you do, in fact, love them. If you can't, don't worry about it. You have plenty of time.

# Basic Goal #3 : Just Whistling in the Dark

## What's the Goal?

Distract yourself when annoyed.

## What's in the Fine Print?

How many times did you successfully distract yourself? "Successfully" means that you choked off yelling or anger before either occurred. You learn to distract yourself by doing something specific; and do the same thing each time you begin to feel annoyed. If you catch yourself before it happens, it won't happen.

- **Although thought is a good place to begin, we can't just think our away into thinness or calmness either.** We can't think our way into long-term behavior change. Sooner or later, we have to do something. Without having mastered yelling and anger, we probably could not master distracting ourselves at the level of annoyance, which is now what needs to be done.

- **We need to work at the more abstract and intellectual part of anger.** Feelings can threaten the work the parent has done so far. That's why there is counseling. Take your feelings to therapy. Work on the actions here. Become aware of those things that seem automatic so that you'll know what you're working with. Then, pick a distraction to help you get past them.

Spike's parents think, "If I don't DO something, the child will think he can get away with murder." First, even if you DO something, Spike will continue to get away with murder because what you do doesn't work. Second, Spike gets away with nothing. His life is a mess. You wouldn't change places with him on a bet. Third, he will learn that you are stronger than he is and, thus, not worth the effort it takes him to be angry.

- **Thus, it is important that when the behavior we call "anger" occurs, we consider the feelings that anger generates.** We learn to override them. We do so through repeated behavior. Feelings are potential threats to our resolve. They gave rise to anger in the past and they could do so again. If feelings are controlled, the likelihood of continued anger expression is increased.

**The easiest way to control the likelihood of yelling or anger is through redirection.** This is a favored technique of the parents of normally developing children. But now you are going to apply it to yourself. Taking a walk is useful. It is hard to exercise and feel anger at the same time. Similarly, scrubbing a floor, building a birdhouse, or weeding the garden will distract. It does not matter what the distraction is, provided it can do two things.

1.  The distraction must be quickly remembered.
2.  The distraction must effectively cause distraction.

The ability to remember the strategy under fire is important. Weeding the garden is good as it is relatively mindless. So is scrubbing the bathroom floor. Neither can hurt you if your mind wanders. Mind wandering is, after all, the intended outcome of allowing oneself to be distracted.

## Is There an Alternative?

If you can't think of anything else, get yourself a hobby. That will help you get your mind away. If your children are the kind who follow you into the bathroom saying, "Why Mommy, why? Why Mommy, why? Why Mommy, why? Why? Why? Why? Why?" stand your ground and put your head on a desert island. Think about the warm breezes. Don't do desert islands? How about ice cream on an August afternoon? Or a roller coaster? Or a mantra? Or recite a prayer? Grab the phone and call your best friend. Make certain it is someone who can actually sympathize with you and not berate you for being a lousy parent. But pick something!

## What's the Last Word?

Living with a tough child is tough, but every day try to do the following in some combination: Look your child in the eye, smile, give a gentle touch, and say something pleasant. And unloving though they may be, see if you can tell them once a week that you do, in fact, love them. If you can't, don't worry about it. You have plenty of time.

"Fair" is a funny word. Spike has no intention of being fair. It is unfair if he doesn't get the whole pie. "Unfair" is when he has to share a piece with you. Some parents also get hung up on "fair" as in, "It's unfair I have to do this program; it's the child who's the troublemaker." Any parent who feels that way can no more finish P.A.C.T. than the man in the moon. "Fair" is irrelevant; concern for a child's future isn't. Learning to distract yourself well means you've gotten beyond that issue.

Know what children like Spike do better than anything in the whole wide world? Split Mom and Dad into raving nut cases, unless, he has already split them into divorce. He knows there is anger and tension, so he slithers between the two and exploits it. He has heard each of them yell to each other, "WHY DON'T YOU DO SOMETHING?!" He also knows there is little respect between them. So, he manipulates the resentment at will. And you know what? They let him!

# The 25 Advanced Goals

**Q:** How do you get to Carnegie Hall?

**A:** Practice, practice, practice.

The basics of the program are now established. If you have learned them well, you are getting paid in changed behavior—your child's and your own. P.A.C.T. relies on repetition. It's good for you. It is intentional and necessary. The strength of the program relies also on its simplicity. The simplicity is stressed often. It is varied in as many different ways as possible because we don't want you to get the impression that you have been trapped inside an echo chamber.

Need an illustration? Just imagine changing light bulbs in the White House. It's a big place. There are lots of light bulbs. They all must be changed. They are, however, all changed in exactly the same way. All clockwise. Repetitive? Redundant? Sure…but what else would you do? Not change some because you get bored easily? You can't afford to be bored. National security depends on your diligence. And there are too many light bulbs that need changing. We're talking the White House here. The guy in charge is fairly influential and you need this credit on your resume. No, you'll change them all because that is what changing light bulbs requires. P.A.C.T., modestly speaking, is your White House. Some of the repeated messages are as follows:

- Detach yourself.
- Don't succumb to impulse.
- Make everything you say sound caring.
- Be responsible only for yourself.
- Have faith in the future.
- Believe in yourself.
- Trust that you taught your child more than he displays.
- Do your best today but know you always have a tomorrow.
- All parents parent the best they know how.
- Doing nothing well beats doing something else poorly.
- Your child loves you but it so happens that neither of you knows it.
- Let your child take the lead.
- Don't worry about being perfect. Tomorrow is a new day.

# CHAPTER 8 : The 25 Advanced Goals

## Advanced Goal #4 : EEEK!

**What's the Goal?**
  Don't get caught by surprise.

**What's in the Fine Print?**
  **Your child surprises you?** By this time in your life, you should understand what makes him tick. You've lived with him day in and day out. You know when he is good. You know when he is bad. Santa Claus has nothing over you.

- **Why should you be in denial about surprises?** You can't accept that his rotten behavior is real. He was a cuddly baby, and he turned into the unhappy thing he is now. You wish it weren't true. You want it to go away. You want a decent, loving family and you haven't got one
- **Too often, a mom will say something like, "I just don't understand what got into him today. He usually isn't like that."**
- **Forget surprise.** You need to be aware that he is a problem. Don't try to take responsibility for his behavior; take responsibility for YOUR behavior. When some child does "A," a parent invariably does "B" and one of the themes of P.A.C.T. is that "B" is almost always self-defeating for you and your child.

> Whenever Spike can catch you unprepared, it's a perverse triumph for him. He doesn't want you prepared and competent. He isn't able to control you then.

- **Plan ahead if you are in the habit of being caught by surprise.** Wake up in the morning and over that first cup of coffee think to yourself, "What is the little darling likely to do today that will piss me off and get me to react? When is he most likely to be so awful that it gets under my skin and I erupt?"

- **Put the times and the situations down on paper.** Be as specific as you can. There probably is little that he hasn't done before and will do again.
- **An unhappy child, having caused our surprise, delights in seeing us stumble and fumble around.** They know that we are trying to be calm as we do our fish-out-of-water routine in the face of something stupid or mean they just did. Flopping around while trying to come up with a solution is comical. Watching that flopping morph into anger is even better. They know the attempt at calmness is likely to be short-lived. They are good at pushing us past our limited tolerance for their nasty behavior. They know we have no fall back except anger or indecision. We simply can't give them the satisfaction of showing either to them,

> Spike's parents used to think he didn't manipulate them with surprise. They thought they were too smart to be tricked. That was then. Now, they know. The moral? The longer it takes a parent to tumble to a child's manipulation, the longer the child is in control. Rotten behavior is all about control. He had it. They didn't.

- **Surprise brings us to splitting.** Your child can come between you and your partner easily. It is called splitting. Your tendency to be caught off guard works to his advantage and against yours. He knows better than you that you have no control and that you two disagree over how to handle him. He has heard you say to your partner: "Do something with that child!" and "Why do you always let him get away with everything?"

As if there really was something either of you could do. Both of you are equally powerless. Both of you are equally frustrated. Parents who work together can't be split. Parents who work together are far less likely to be caught by surprise because this child has become a joint project. These children are very good at getting their parents to divorce, by the way. Often, the father says he can't stand it anymore and leaves.

Nobody likes surprises, unless they are birthday parties. We like to know what is coming. Living with your child has made a mockery of order. Now you can see negative family patterns and adjust

> How does Spike control? He sets the tone for the household by getting everything to revolve around him. He makes himself unpredictable, so everyone tip-toes on eggshells until they can't stand it anymore. He, thus, imposes conditions for your happiness by being hard to manage. You are repeatedly thrown on the defensive. So, you fight fire with fire, and he holds the extinguisher.

accordingly. Surprise is nothing more than a lack of planning. It should not characterize your life with your child. If splitting continues, it is because one parent sees themselves as superior to the other and refuses to cooperate.

.

**What's the Last Word?**

Living with a tough child is tough, but every day try to do the following in some combination: Look your child in the eye, smile, give a gentle touch, and say something pleasant. And unloving though they may be, see if you can tell them once a week that you do, in fact, love them. If you can't, don't worry about it. Some day you may be able to. You have plenty of time.

Lily Tomlin said, "Man invented language to satisfy his deep need to complain," which turns out to be a huge waste of time.

Most of P.A.C.T. is about language. Language, which is to say, our need to talk about how unhappy we are, is a trap. Save it for therapy.

Got An Angry Kid?

# Advanced Goal #5 : "If You Do That One More Time!"

**What's the Goal?**
   Don't threaten.

**What's in the Fine Print?**
   **Threatening the over-sensitive is an invitation for a tantrum.** The miserable child is a sensitive child. Over-sensitivity is a prevailing symptom of how he feels about himself. He is apprehensive about anything that looks, tastes or feels like rejection. He lives on a knife edge and no matter which way he turns, he cuts himself.

"Spike? Time for dinner."
"Quit yer nagging! That's all I ever hear. Spike this, Spike that. I can't stand it. I'll eat when I want to."

- **Spike easily takes offense; threatening him is high on the list.** He sees threat everywhere, even in the sound of your breathing.
- **His sensitivity has made you hyper-cautious.** You have gotten yourself into the habit of walking around on eggshells because you are afraid this child is going to flip out. The eggshells will go away as you understand the calculus of your reaction and his sensitivity.
- **Parents promote the likelihood that their child will present them with a behavioral crisis by threatening them.** Avoid saying: "I'm gonna ground you if you don't clean up your room." "Big deal!" "I mean it!!" "Drop dead bitch."
- **The first problem with threatening is that it is a challenge.** The miserable child feels cornered. He isn't likely to let a challenge go without a counter-challenge. The second problem is that he doesn't care. The third problem is that he doesn't believe the threat. The fourth problem is that parents reveal to Spike more of their inability to control him. The fifth problem is that Spike says things he shouldn't say to a parent without consequence. Considering one's options, the best path to follow when considering threat is: DON'T.

- **Threat has nothing to recommend it.** If you have something you wish your child to do, be direct and ask for it if, but only if, you think he will do it. When dealing with a miserable child, parents must learn to make choices. They can't achieve everything they want with their child. He won't let them. Parents must decide on those things that are important to them and let everything else ride.

- **How important is it for him to clean his room which is never cleaned?** Or do school work, which is never done anyhow; or speak nicely to his sister which also never happens? Some things can be postponed. Spike won't live in filth for the rest of his life. But being a slob is now a matter of pride. That is a lot for Mom to overcome, especially during unhappy times when his room, looking like the town dump, glares back at her. So she falls back on toothless threat. Not wise.

> There is no advantage in one parent displaying contempt for the other in front of the child. No matter what an idiot Spike's Mom thinks his Dad is, seeing him humiliated is the last thing that little Spike needs. Resentments aside, if you value your child more than your own irritation, you will keep contempt to yourself. Otherwise, you will look like as big a loser as the parent you are undercutting.

- **The parent who insists on a certain level of cleanliness** will have a challenge taking all of her resources to get the job done. She is encouraged to let him live in his own squalor. If your pet peeve is closing the front door in winter as Junior has failed to do for the umpteenth time, as in: "SHUT THE GODDAMNED DOOR!! HOW MANY TIMES DO I HAVE TO TELL YOU! IF I HAVE TO COME OVER THERE…."

- **The parent should: (1) stop with the mouth; (2) wait for Spike to leave the house; or (3) get off the couch and quietly, without fanfare, ceremony, or noise gently close the door behind him.** DON'T SLAM IT. We don't want the little miscreant to know you did it. But the door got closed and there were no hot words. Is this a violation of your parental rights? Yes, but so what? It's strategy. Will you spend the rest of your natural life closing the front door after him? No. This is all part of the process. If you feel you need to say anything, instead of a threat, make the request simple and direct, like: "It's time to clean the room."

- **It doesn't mean, of course, that Spike will respect this any more than he will the other requests but at least it isn't a threat.** Many of the goals presented in this program are not cataclysmic. But each one is a piece of the puzzle. So saying, "I need the room cleaned" represents an improvement. One of the two most important things to be gained from P.A.C.T. is parental self-control. If the parent can be civil in the face of unpleasantness, another brick has been added. The other most important feature is control of the child. Forget the beatings. They will get you arrested if the child doesn't turn on you and beat you first.

- **There may be no consequence, including threatening, that motivates this child.** Threats delivered to the emotionally disturbed child are toothless. Not only is this frustrating to parents, but it leads to anger about ineffectiveness. Children should not be exposed to parental ineffectiveness. If the only thing the parent can control is themselves, then they must be content.

- **Misery is a contest in which the victor (Spike) manipulates the loser (Mom and Dad) into irrelevance and sputtering fury because they relied on pointless techniques such as threatening.** To the extent that a child remains a problem, he continues to be the winner. In the short term, he has the upper hand and his parents are continually outmaneuvered. Generals have strategies for use on the battlefield So should parents.

- **Since threatening is just one more example of giving control back to the child, eliminate it.** Contests can't work if one member refuses to play. Most likely, Spike will gradually stop and go home.

By controlling threats, parents control the outcome of the match. If we think of a serve as a verbal volley, there is practically nothing that a parent can "serve"—not threats, not preaching, not sarcasm, not anything—that will be effective. Ineffectiveness is precisely the opposite image that a parent needs his miserable child to see.

Dad has an easier time with Spike than Mom. Mom is flexible. Mom wipes the nose and smears on the sympathy. Dad isn't much good around feelings. Both threaten a lot. Both get nowhere. Flexibility is Mom's undoing; it means mom and dad are on different pages. Mom says, "You don't understand; it's a mommy thing." Dad says, "You don't understand; the kid is a pain in the neck." Spike understands, too. He gets Mom to hate dad really fast. Dad says he can see this kid coming a mile away and Mom can't. Both end up very resentful.

## Is There an Alternative?

The reverse of threatening is giving a warning. Don't do it unless it is successful for you. Don't say, "If you do XYZ, I'm gonna do ABC." Rather, give a polite request, wait a reasonable period for compliance and then supply a consequence if you have a meaningful one. They actually don't need a warning. They've had a lifetime of them, and they don't believe you. If you don't have a consequence that works, don't even ask in the first place. Postpone asking for a few weeks until things start to calm down

## What's the Last Word?

Living with a tough child is tough, but every day try to do the following in some combination: Look your child in the eye, smile, give a gentle touch, and say something pleasant. And unloving though they may be, see if you can tell them once a week that you do, in fact, love them. If you can't, don't worry about it. Some day you may be able to. You have plenty of time.

Henry Louis Mencken said, "Conscience is the inner voice that says somebody is listening."

P.A.C.T. says, conscience for Spike exists, it just happens to be buried under a whole lot of crud, and it listens poorly until his parents give him reason to listen.

# Advanced Goal #6 : "Why you (bleep, bleep) little (bleep)!"

"Eat shit and die."

—a morning greeting from an anonymous adolescent

## What's the Goal?

Don't swear.

## What's in the Fine Print?

**We could start by listing common swears as a way of calling the Devil by his name.** It would begin the process of demystifying cursing. But we don't need to. We all know what they are. Children use them on us all the time. We use them on children, too.

- **Why talk about child's swearing when it is the parent's obligation to get rid of theirs?** It makes for nice illustration. If you come to see swearing as ridiculous in your child, imagine what it looks like in you.
- **Swearing should produce a yawn, not high blood pressure.** Children aren't very imaginative when it comes to swearing. Turns out adults aren't either. Everyone uses the same half-dozen curses.
- **There is something about oath uttering that seems to be empowering.** Why it is we let others, especially children, empower themselves at our expense by swearing is a bit of a mystery since most of it is nonsense. Paying attention at all is nuts. If a child says to you: "Go to Hell!" will it actually occur?

The swearing goal is not intended to turn parents into prudes. How dull. Instead, it's part of an effort for parents to get control over themselves. Thus, when the occasion arises (after P.A.C.T. has concluded, of course) and looks like cursing could be spectacularly joyous, do it. But by then you will understand why you do it and why you don't. Then you can be selective.

One of the things that this program can say to you without reservation is that your child can't send you to hell. He can make you feel as though you live in it, but that is another story. The power of swearing lies in the meaning of swearing that YOU or someone attaches to it. As in, "You son of a bitch!" he says to his brother. "Oh, my God," Mother says, overhearing the exchange, "He thinks I'm a bitch."

Well, no. The "bitch" part is just an expression, perhaps not a nice one, but an expression just the same. You are both free to notice or to find beneath your notice.

- **If you're worried that people think that you're a terrible mom, so what?** They probably already do. Don't worry about them. They aren't raising that devil of a child; you are.
- **If you don't think you could stand the embarrassment, is it the embarrassment of being sworn at or the embarrassment of ignoring it?** Just one of them is in your direct control and it is not the first one.
- **Swearing is one of those human impulses that people dislike in others but tolerate in themselves.** But since life is generally unfair, we all feel the need to compete on whatever level is handy. Swearing is a bonding agent used by the boys down at the plant. Maybe the girls, too. It may not be nice, but it is relatively harmless. It is used for shock value. But, honestly, swearing at a child is like shooting a mouse with an elephant gun. It confers far too much status on the mouse.
- **But whether swearing seems tough or not, it is a constant in the lives of most out-of-control children.** They learned somewhere along the line that the shock value swearing gets when adults use it is at least as good as the shock value they get when they use it. The more offended we are at hearing it, the more they will use it against us, and the more we are likely to reciprocate.
- **"Fuck you" is now the coin of the realm.** But just because something is universal does not mean it's acceptable and everyone knows it, including children. Children in normal settings don't use such language against their parents. Children in angered settings do.
- **Swearing back at a foul-mouthed child serves no purpose except to show that the parents' lack of imagination is equal to that of their children.** Children who swear at their parents will swear at anyone including teachers and potential bosses should one of them loom large enough in their lives to become a problem.

Since we all know that swearing is bad, why do we do it? It's cheap. It's handy. It's thoughtless. It works. There is, by the way, a distinction between being sworn at and sworn around. The first is bad and the second is tasteless. If you concentrate on the first, the second will go away, too.

## What's the Last Word?

Living with a tough child is tough, but every day try to do the following in some combination: Look your child in the eye, smile, give a gentle touch, and say something pleasant. And unloving though they may be, see if you can tell them once a week that you do, in fact, love them. If you can't, don't worry about it. Some day you may be able to. You have plenty of time.

# Advanced Goal #7 : "I declare, butter would melt in her mouth."

Change your tone of voice.

## What's in the Fine Print?

**The hypersensitive child feeds off your tone of voice.** Spike will look for and find all instances of perceived criticism. He will turn them back on his mom and dad. He can find a lot of it in their tone of voice. We carry everything we feel in tone. It is like a suitcase that refuses to stay in the attic.

- **"Tone" behaves according to some well-established principles.** Learning theory tells us that the better something is learned (i.e., swearing at parents, swiping candy bars, hitting sisters), (1) the more resistant it is to being forgotten; (2) the more it is likely to influence other similar things; and (3) the easier it is to maintain.

Swiping candy bars is a good example because many children do it at least once, and some do it a great deal. Stealing is a selfish act. It says, this is mine, I deserve it, and I get it. I don't care how others feel.

Tone operates the same way. Let's break tone and swiping down—a child who swipes candy bars without consequence is a child who may continue to swipe. The more the child swipes, the more automatic it becomes. Same for tone: if there is no inhibitor to someone's nasty tone, it easily endures.

Since swiping candy is, for this child, a by-product of anger, swiping may become attached to other instances of anger besides chocolate. Similarly, we get away with having a terrible tone of voice in which everything we feel gets broadcast because there is no consequence that we accept. Soon, grouchiness in one area becomes grouchiness in another. It turns into a way of life.

We end up sounding worse, not better just as the child may end up stealing more, not less. The parent may report that her child is stealing all the time. Since there are many events in this child's life that cause him anger, he may gradually use them to justify stealing or sounding awful.

Tone of voice mirrors everything.

- **What to do about tone?** Become aware of your tone. Change it. Practice until the changes are automatic. Tone change is ultimately an attitude, not a set of rules. P.A.C.T.'s goals are a means to achieve the attitude, not an end, in themselves. P.A.C.T. wants your feeling for the tone to be spontaneous, automatic, and unthinking and it will, with practice.
- **Thusfar, in addition to tone, the parents have eliminated yelling, anger, feelings of annoyance and threats.** This is a huge accomplishment. Parents would not be at this point in the program if they didn't already see change. But the change is fragile. All the old goals must be practiced every day, along with the newly added ones.
- **Will Spike interpret a parent's hostile tone of voice as anything other than rejection?** No. Will he give himself permission to continue stealing because his parents are jerks anyway, so it doesn't matter what he does? Yes. If we want him to stop stealing and all the other bad things he does, we can't approach him directly.
- **A change in our tone is designed to get Spike to accept the reality of his own destructive unhappiness and change.** The change occurs by stealth. It will happen in a way that he does not recognize. Your positive tone will signal acceptance. He will build on it.
- **Tone becomes a weapon but of a very different kind. A contest with drawn pistols is out of the question.** Tone of voice may seem small, but then most of the things that maintain misery are small. An unkind word one day, a perceived slight the next. It doesn't take much. It doesn't take much for an adult to react, either. A parent may say, "I don't have to walk around on tip-toes for my other children, why do I have to for this one?"
- **Children differ; accept it.** Adjust how you sound. You think that because there are several children in the family that you raised the same, talked to the same, dressed the same that they will behave the same? It is not true. They are all different and Spike is REALLY different. Your tone with Spike has been different, too.

In the meantime, it is sufficient to say that the unhappy child's sensitivity must be addressed if he is to be changed. Tone of voice is a way of addressing sensitivity. For parents who are uncertain about their tone of voice, they may wish to have another adult listen to them. But if they remember things like speaking with kindness, politeness, and respectfulness, even in the face of disrespect, they will do well.

## What's the Last Word?

Living with a tough child is tough, but every day try to do the following in some combination: Look your child in the eye, smile often, give a gentle touch, and say something pleasant. And unloving though they may be, see if you can tell them once a week that you do, in fact, love them. If you can't, don't worry about it. Some day you may be able to.

The great American philosopher Rodney Dangerfield said, "I told my psychiatrist that everyone hates me; he said, 'Nonsense…everyone hasn't met you yet.'"

P.A.C.T. says, the biggest impediment to completing P.A.C.T. is self confidence. Spike's parents haven't much self confidence about their parenting. Why would they? But, that is now about to change. If you look in the mirror and the mirror tells you you're ugly, get a new mirror.

Ruff likes Angelique about as much as Spike does.

# Advanced Goal #8 : "Yeah, right… What are you, the (bleep)ing Queen?"

## What's the Goal?
No sarcasm.

## What's in the Fine Print?

Sarcasm is rude. It has a nasty little hook on the end. Its nastiness lies in its wit. Sarcasm can be amusing among friends, but between parent and miserable child, it's not. The child doesn't get the joke. Well, that isn't exactly true. He is the joke and at some level, knows it.

- **Sarcasm is a manipulation of language.** We think we are clever when sarcastic. We play with words and meanings. Sarcasm gets a chuckle, but not from the victim. Often the intent of child-directed sarcasm is to be mean, not amusing. It produces a sharp reaction. Our over-sensitive Spike can't "just take a joke" because he is "so thin-skinned." "Well I can see you spent hours cleaning up this dump." Mom says surveying Spike's room. "Maybe you are eligible for a toxic waste grant." "Mommy," he says in return, "Go fuck yourself!"
- **This isn't a chapter ripped from *Rebecca of Sunnybrook Farm*.** Surely Rebecca wouldn't stoop to sarcasm, nor can we imagine her being cursed at. What has been accomplished by this interchange? Nothing, except the likelihood that it will happen again. Mommy has reduced herself to the Spike's level. Spike is giving it right back to her by answering the only way he can. The longer Spike is convinced that his mom's sarcasm is the reason why he is grumpy, the longer he will go without cleaning his room, or anything else.
- **Mom is the safe deposit box for Spike's anger.** She is allowing anger, through her sarcasm, to happen. Parents who permit this transfer of responsibility from child to parent and do not change it when given the opportunity are asking for continued trouble.
- **The emotionally disturbed child should not be allowed to get away with targeting his anger at parents.** They aren't likely to handle it well. Parents are about the only people a child can torture and get away with it. Parents are the ones who, no matter what, will take you in, forgive you, give you $5, and lie about you. Parents are historically lousy guardians

of their child's anger. The idea of detaching themselves from it doesn't occur to them and, if it did, they would probably feel guilty because parents are supposed, to somehow feel their child's pain.

- **Sarcasm is a mutual event.** Depends on how pissed Mom is at Spike. Sarcasm is as much in the ear of the beholder as it is in the lips of a sender. Almost anything can be interpreted as sarcasm by the hypersensitive.
- **Removing sarcasm will not necessarily get Spike's room clean.** In fact, nothing except his mother may get his roomed cleaned. Room cleaning may not be an important battle to pick. You may want to go in from time to time to retrieve the dirty dishes or dispose of food rotting under the bed. But if a cleaning is something you can live without, swallow hard and drop the subject. Do even normally developing children have clean rooms? Only those on TV. Another possibility is to do it yourself and say nothing. Absolutely nothing. Especially nothing sarcastic. The issue shouldn't become a pointless tug-of-war. If you can stand it trashed, leave it alone. The impulse to fling a parting bit of sarcasm is overwhelming to some. Don't let it be to you.

## Is There an Alternative?

Stop and think, or have a practiced alternative statement that is positive even though it is unlikely to be accepted. Say out loud, "A little mouse for want of stairs/ran up a rope to say its prayers." This is short, memorable, and just nutty enough to drive your child into the next room. It is also utterly harmless and couldn't convey sarcasm if it wanted. Your child will think you are crazy, but then, he does already, so big deal.

## What's the Last Word?

Living with a tough child is tough, but every day try to do the following in some combination: Look your child in the eye, smile, give a gentle touch, and say something pleasant. And unloving though they may be, see if you can tell them once a week that you do, in fact, love them. If you can't, don't worry about it. Some day you may be able to. You have plenty of time.

# Advanced Goal #9 : "What's with the earring? You gay or something?"

## What's the Goal?
No criticism.

## What's in the Fine Print?
**We live in a critical culture.** Conventional success is paramount. Failure is contemptible. Failure is shameful, especially the failure of childrearing. Nothing, reflects so fundamentally on parents as the success or failure of their child. Riches are nothing.

Everyone is a critic. Schoolwork is graded. Baseball has winners and losers. The pressure to succeed can be tough even among normally progressing individuals. Poorly progressive children are in trouble. We are forever asking others around us, "Which one did you like the best?"

Somebody or something has to come out on top. It doesn't matter if we are talking tennis shoes or pasta. Indifference is not a choice. We must prove ourselves over and over. Almost everyone, our parents included, take us only on condition. We follow the rules of the most important people in our lives until we decide their rules aren't worth the effort. At that point, in the child's view, the camel's back has been broken. Too many conditions are required. He isn't playing the game any more.

Some children are exposed to more punishment than most, and don't handle it as well. The ability to cope develops poorly when exposure to criticism occurs in early childhood. Children are made weaker, not stronger, by exposure to criticism. A child can be exposed to a pressure-provoking experience. The event may have little or no negative effect if he or she is with a nurturing adult during the experience. But if the adult isn't nurturing, watch out.

The vital piece is the parent. Let's say your child rakes the lawn. You didn't ask him to. He didn't announce his plans. He just did. How do you react? Do you say, "You missed a spot!" Or do you say, "Thanks."

We recommend the latter, but the former is common. P.A.C.T. parents find that, much to their surprise, their child will spontaneously perform good deeds. When it happens, don't overdue the praise. But don't ignore the child's impulse either.

- **Don't like the job he did on the leaves?** Acknowledge the attempt. Live with the results, or re-do it yourself. Just forget the editorializing. Accept what you can get and be grateful. One thing is vital: never criticize a vulnerable child.
- **Criticism is pressure.** It weakens a child's self respect. CHILDREN learn to react to criticism with anger. They know little about why they feel badly. They do know that they feel bad. Nothing they do is good enough, smart enough, kind enough, brave enough, or special enough to get away from the pressure of people who are disappointed in them. They escape into depression or aggression.
- **The unhappy child is a sensitive child who can not tolerate the least criticism.** Spike will project his unhappiness back onto the most important people in his life, his parents. He will refuse (by his actions) to take responsibility for his feelings and actions. Parents who criticize are this child's foil. Their criticism is more confirmation that they find him inadequate. He will not budge so long as they find him inadequate.

Eliminating criticism is implied in most program goals. The overall objective is to remove criticism in all its forms. While only the unhappy child can change his own disposition, the parent's role is to create the conditions under which that change will occur.

> Somewhere, we fell into the trap of believing that constructive criticism is a good thing; that even the miserable ought to profit by it. Well, he can't distinguish between good criticism and bad. It's all bad to him. He hasn't the self-confidence to see the difference.

## Is There an Alternative?

The reverse of criticism is praise. These children have a hard time hearing praise and believing praise. If you can find something about him/her to praise, try it but focus on the object, not the child. "The floor looks nice, thanks," as opposed to "You did a nice job on the floor, thanks." Taking him/her out of "the" means he doesn't filter it through himself, which he will find insincere.

## What's the Last Word?

Living with a tough child is tough, but every day try to do the following in some combination: Look your child in the eye, smile, give a gentle touch, and say something pleasant. And, unloving though they may be, see if you can tell them once a week that you do, in fact, love them. If you can't, don't worry about it. Some day you may be able to. You have plenty of time.

# Advanced Goal #10 : "Don't make me repeat myself!"

**What's the Goal?**
No nagging.

**What's in the Fine Print?**
**Nagging is a loaded term.** It is not politically correct. It describes a traditional mother/wife. She is reminding her errant child/husband of some limitation to their obligations and competence. But children call the exchange "nagging," which is reflection of how they feel about it. Political correctness is a luxury in family wars.

> "Did you clean your room?"
> "Are you sure you cleaned your room?"
> "If I go upstairs, will I see a clean room?"
> "If I've asked you once, I've asked you a dozen times, did you clean your room?"
> "I hate to keep asking, but did you clean your room?"
> "So how's the room?"
> "Your room is a pigsty. You should be ashamed, it's so bad."

- **Nagging sucks.** The surest way never to get that room cleaned is to repeatedly raise the subject.
- **Mothers, quite naturally, are not fond of the term "nagging."** Moreover, since they have general charge of the house and children, the responsibility for having things done falls to them. It's mothers who get hunted down when things go wrong. They bristle at being blamed for their child's failure.
- **Creating a miserable child is often a group effort.** Maybe the father's idea of a meaningful relationship ended with his child's conception. Maybe he deserted when things got tough. Maybe he still hangs around but contributes little other than a check. Whatever the reason, Mom often gets left holding the bag.
- **Nagging needs to be eliminated for the same reason so many other things need to be**

eliminated: **it is ineffective.** Regardless of the politics or how our child got to be the way he is, we will no longer take the responsibility for his unhappiness, except to make our life, and by extension his life, better. We will increase the likelihood that he will want to change. We will creating a non-threatening atmosphere.

Nagging a child, or an adult for that matter, over and over to accomplish some task may actually get it done. Even if it works, it requires a huge expenditure of effort. It generates such ill will that it snuffs out potential cooperation. Nagging uses precious ammunition to accomplish something small. Nagging does not give the impression of strength, even though in some hands it can be as insistent as an iron pipe. Better to turn that effort into something useful.

## Is There an Alternative?

If it needs to be done, do it yourself. If you can afford to leave it alone, leave it alone. If it is really important to you, use a consequence that reliably works. If you must get your child out of bed, then say, "get up" without sounding anything other than neutral. Say it again. Keep your voice the same. Say it again. Keep your voice at the same neutral level. Say it again. And again. And again. Become a drone. Say it again. Show NO emotion. It will work.

How many times do we need to repeat something before our monster says we are nagging? Often, once will do. Nagging is clearly in the ear of the beholder.

## What's the Last Word?

Living with a tough child is tough, but every day try to do the following in some combination: Look your child in the eye, smile often, give a gentle touch, and say something pleasant. And unloving though they may be, see if you can tell them once a week that you do, in fact, love them. If you can't, don't worry about it. Some day you may be able to. You have plenty of time.

# Advanced Goal #11 : "If you do that again, you're grounded for six months."

## What's the Goal?

Follow-through.

## What's in the Fine Print?

There are few things that inspire less respect in parents than telling a child that he is grounded **and not doing it**. It is not a good idea to paint yourself into a corner by asserting something you won't do. You say you will ground Spike for six months? Really? It is an impossibly long time. How about 24 hours? Seriously. Your child is probably used to your irrational threats. He assumes they are bogus. Most anyone can pull off a 24-hour grounding. Nobody can last six months. If you CAN'T pull off a 24-hour grounding, why are you threatening six months??

There are two common results to threats or demands that are not enforced (aka, poor follow-through): You show ineffectiveness, and your child escapes without consequences. You both lose, but you lose more because you have given away your self-respect to a child who manipulates you into irrationality and learns to walk away.

The rule throughout P.A.C.T., including follow-through, is that if any of your parenting techniques do not work, dump them. The best way is not to threaten consequences in the first place. Barring that, if you have a short-term consequence in mind that your child will respect before this same child drags you into conflict, use it. Preplanning is important. Keep it simple. Pick battles you can win. But if you declare you intend to do something, you are compelled to do it.

> Follow-through will cure you from saying something outrageous. But just in case you get carried away, your punishment is, "if you say it, you do it." Spike already thinks you're a fraud. Going back on what you say just confirms it.

Do you ever get to relax and let the child off the follow-through hook? Not for a long time. Let him get used to you having standards. If you can't impose standards, do not attempt them. If the standard you impose fails, do not attempt it again until you have reasonable certainly that it will work. Opportunities will present themselves. Time is on the side of the parent who is attempting to create change. Do not listen to the well-intended neighbor or relative who, in the midst of your struggle, says: "If that child were mine, I'd take a belt to him. You coddle him, that's your problem."

Most people have not been where you are. Many people have been where you are and are still there. Neither are much use to you. They're stuck. Either they don't have a child anything like yours or they refuse to see a relationship between how they feel and act and how their children feel and act. As one unsuccessful client whose 10-year-old child was finally removed by the state, once said, "This child is amoral. No morals. NONE. He is selfish and mean. And I will not lower myself to his level. If that is the way he wants to be, then that is his decision. I know right from wrong, and I insist that he follow my standards. Why, even his grandfather hates him. I give up. I don't know what to do."

This client had been told what to do and had ample time to do it. Her child thumbed his nose at her. Her attempts at control were limited to complaining. Her son was a challenge; selfish to be sure, but he was far from amoral. She wanted a lightning bolt to strike, punishing the child for not being as virtuous as she was. She didn't think it was her job to teach her child. So she didn't.

Follow-through is caring. It means you are willing to inconvenience yourself to do what needs to be done. Self-righteous sputtering was all the mom above could muster. When it got right down to it, this woman didn't like her child. It's no wonder she couldn't get any traction.

One of the several things that the mother above refused to do was follow-through. She couldn't avoid putting both of them in an unwinable situation. She insisted on a task that she knew from experience would fail. She said, "I tell him not to do something, and he does it anyway! I tell him to mind his manners, and he eats with his mouth open. He sits at the table and makes disgusting sounds. I tell him to respect his sister's room, and he rummages through it. Why should I have to put a bolt on the door just because he thinks he can do what he wants? I tell him to stay away from my computer, and he gets to it when I'm not looking and does God knows what. And then when I tell him he has been bad and there will be no ice cream, he goes ballistic and swears and threatens. It's terrible."

> Controlling personalities struggle with the flexibility that P.A.C.T. requires. They can be rigid, sure of themselves to a fault, perfectionists, addicted to routine, and risk adverse. They may be successful so long as they stick to narrow and well-rehearsed interests. During good times, they are handy, if annoying, to have around. During bad times, they are part of the problem because they don't give an inch and can rationalize their whacked-out biases until the cows come home.

The follow-through picture that begins to emerge here is a mother who is long on telling her child what do and short on developing a strategy to achieve it. All we see are words. We don't see self-restraint. We see complaining about how tough things are. Training a child takes time, patience and love. Those involved with this mom and child came to the conclusion that she had too little of the latter to do what she needed to do to make this child safe. And both failed. The problem of poor follow-through is based on a simple equation: Action = Reaction = Counter-reaction

Or, in other words, parent does something, child does something in response and parent trumps that with some action. The action should be so well understood that it anticipates what the reaction will be. In unhappy homes it is:

Mom (Action): "Don't eat with your mouth open"
Child (Reaction): "Up yours!"
Mom (Counter-reaction): "No ice cream for you."

Most of the clients that come to P.A.C.T. are moms. P.A.C.T. is successful with dads, too, but dads are more likely than moms to give up and wash their hands of the whole mess.

Most children soon get the picture that their parents are a constant in a strong, predictable way. Parents always have an ace up their sleeve: They always have the ability to say, "NO" when Junior asks for something. But, having said, "NO," they'd better stick to it.

If you use your head, follow-through is not a big deal. "So, what's this woman's problem?" someone may ask. "The child is going to react and if you refuse to have an effective counter-reaction (complaining about him isn't one of them), why set him up in the first place? What have you gained? What has he gained? You either have something to follow through with or you drop the subject."

But the mother mentioned above was stuck. Time and again she shook her verbal finger, then was outraged when her child swore back at her. She saw her role as strictly that of admonisher and thought it should be sufficient.

She had no interest in the follow-through. Her admonishments were implied threats. She served the tennis ball. It was up to her 10-year-old to get it back to her the way she wanted without her having to fret about the details. Her consequences ("No ice cream tonight!") were insignificant. The fact that he would blow off her counter-reaction is part of what led her to believe that he was amoral. Unhappy people can't be bought off. They want the real thing, and it was probably becoming apparent to this child that he was not going to get the real thing: love, patience, and acceptance.

We think it's our birthright to pass on everything we know about life whether Spike asks us or not. A normal child can put up with it, but not an out-of-control child. We parents of these latter children have no credibility and, thus, have absolutely nothing of worth to say on any subject. Moral: Keep it to yourself unless asked.

## Is There an Alternative?

If you slip and tell your child that you are removing a privilege for a month or two, take out a calendar and write it down. Stick to it. Parents forget, and children count on their forgetting.

## What's the Last Word?

Living with a tough child is tough, but every day try to do the following in some combination: Look your child in the eye, smile, give a gentle touch, and say something pleasant. And unloving though they may be, see if you can tell them once a week that you do, in fact, love them. If you can't, don't worry about it. Some day you may be able to. You have plenty of time.

Mark Twain said,
"Man is the only
animal that blushes…
or needs to."

P.A.C.T. says, blushing
is something we miss
in Spike. He leads
some of us to think he
hasn't any morals or
any humility. He does.
He has plenty of both.
Too much, in fact, of
the latter. He just won't
show you.

# Advanced Goal #12 : "When I Was Your Age..."

**What's in the Fine Print?**

   **Preaching is a fine old occupation.** There is a drone that is associated with preaching from the pulpit. There is another that comes from the front parlor. Parents assume that if they get on their soapbox and intone a moral lesson, Spike will eventually listen. No, he won't. The parent is preaching to himself. Spike tuned out a long time ago. As far as the children like Spike are concerned, parents have nothing to say. Period. Parents need to understand this.

   Preaching is what parents do, isn't it? Not with Spike they don't. You may say, "But I don't feel like a parent if I can't give him guidance." But the time for that has passed. Move on. Tend to your own needs. He will attend to his, although not as well as you would like. Not that it matters since you don't have much choice.

   Preaching, lecturing, and giving unwanted/unsolicited advice all emerge from the same place: tradition. Parents have a tradition of authoritarianism. It is hopelessly dated. The Victorian papa went the way of the Dodo. Back in the day when you needed the old man's permission to marry, he (and the rest of the family) had certain expectations about the weight of his authority. Doubtless, Victorians produced their share of unhappy children, too. Traditions of fatherhood notwithstanding, they would have been well advised to cut out the lecturing, too. Simply because it is old does not make it good. If those guys in mutton chops were sensible, they did.

> You say you are going to give a moral lecture to someone who thinks you are terrible? What can you be thinking? If the tables were turned, would you listen?

   The real issue in lecturing is the unsolicited issue. You are free to lecture yourself into tomorrow if your child gives you permission. One thing all parents who learn P.A.C.T. experience is that their child will, in fact, come to them for advice. But they won't accept it in a lecture. Spike's solicitations seem far-fetched from this vantage, but they will happen. Your child does want you. In that event, keep the message short. Be grateful that he asks your opinion. Reward his progress by being brief. Give him the chance to ask again.

For now, you need to accept the fact that your child really does not like you. It is probably temporary but, even so, it is real. Once you can accept this fact, you can accept the fact that nothing associated with you is desirable in this child's eyes, save your wallet. (Although even there, he is likely to take your $5 and then accuse you of trying to buy him. This one is hard to win.) Anything else associated with you will be rejected. Allow this child the opportunity to reject you without comment. If you can get used to it, he will cut it out. He will be back and it won't take forever.

## Is There an Alternative?

If you have a need to deliver a sermon and now understand that you can't, have someone else do it. This is fairly risky since one preaching adult is interchangeable with the next, but if you can find someone that he trusts, enlist that other person. It is possible that such a person is the juvenile justice officer in your town. It might be a neighbor or teacher.

## What's the Last Word?

Living with a tough child is tough, but every day try to do the following in some combination: Look your child in the eye, smile, give a gentle touch, and say something pleasant. And unloving though they may be, see if you can tell them once a week that you do, in fact, love them. If you can't, don't worry about it. Some day you may be able to. You have plenty of time.

# Advanced Goal #13 : "Mommy? If I clean up my room can I have $5…huh?"

**What's the Goal?**
  Don't make deals.

**What's in the Fine Print?**
  Deals are for rug traders, not for nasty little children who live to make their parents miserable. Don't fall for it. It's a set-up

  Problem #1: Mommy's certain that Spike is as sincere as she. She loves him. She knows he's having a hard life. She wants to help. She feels vulnerable whenever he comes to her with that gee-whiz voice of his and asks for something. But he isn't sincere. It's an act. Sure, you are ever the sweet Mommy who is trying to show her child that there is a special bond between you two. You bend over backward to seem fair. But, you know what? The more you bend, the more Spike pushes. And fair? What is this "fair" stuff? We've already discussed that Spike's sense of fair can only be satisfied when he has the whole pie. Fair is what happens when you go without. Think we have this wrong? Tell him, "NO" and see what happens. If you are only sworn at, you get off lightly.

  Why should that be? Because way down deep where he can't express himself, Spike thinks that everything has been taken from him and he is left with nothing. The cupboard is bare. So taking the entire pie makes sense. The least you can do, from his vantage, to make things right is not complain about it. He will do what he can, including being devious, to get what he needs. He will distort what he can to make it seem reasonable. He will always outwit you because he will always push things further that you will. You know when to stop. He doesn't. Well, he may know but he doesn't care.

  Deals are only made to be broken. That is exactly what will happen. You think you have agreement because Spike shakes his head. Don't be naïve. Spike has no intention of holding up his end of the bargain, and you should know better than to think he will. He rarely has in the past unless it is tied immediately to something he wants. He sure isn't about to keep the bargain just for you.

  At best, the deal will be a half-assed effort. You will predictably end up frustrated. You will say something like, "If you clean the garage, sweetheart, I'll give you $5." Lets assume he is desperate for the $5 so he actually agrees. Sometime later, he says he is finished.

"Are you sure?" you say to him. "Did you get the in corners?"
"Oh, ,Ma, of course I did. Now I gotta go…gimme the $5, okay?"

You foolishly give it to him. Then, you go to the garage and see that he did a sloppy job. This would be the same story if he raked the leaves, mowed the grass, took out the garbage or fed the dog. He will not ever hold up his end of the bargain. Ever. Count on it. Assume it.

All of your deals will be similar: (1) Both of you will agree; (2) He will do a lousy job; and (3)There will be a ruckus over $5. Sooner or later, you will wise up, you will resist, and that will be his clue to get mean. He put you in a corner where you must be on top of him to see that he gets the agreed-upon job done. It is a game. It is exhausting for the parent. You are rushing around to see that he is compliant with something he agreed to do. He knew he was just blowing you off. The wrong person is doing the running around. Running must be transferred to Spike. How is that done? By NEVER agreeing to a deal. He can't make one with you. You can't make one with him.

Problem #2: Reliability. Every time you let Spike off the hook, he just believes you are infinitely flexible in all the wrong ways. He can walk up one side of you and down the other. He knows if he comes to you and says, "Ma, if I wash the car, can I have $5?" All he has to do is turn on the hose, and the $5 is his. He knows he can rely on you to be wishy-washy. You don't want that. You have exposed your soft underbelly to a carnivore. Don't kid yourself, this child has teeth. You may as well break out the steak sauce. It means you are not reliable. It means whatever you say is subject to negotiation later. So why should he ever have to enter a negotiation honestly? Or listen to you? He knows he does not need to. He can resort to whining, begging, or any other obnoxious thing and break down your will. Why would you bargain away your credibility. That's what you are doing. Making deals is both desperate and weak. Stick to your guns. Don't bargain.

**Is There an Alternative?**

Be highly selective. Don't enter into any relationship without certainly that you will prevail. Only ask for things you can enforce. Only ask for things you will get. If you don't get it, next time don't ask. But don't set yourself up to be undermined by the wily deal maker. He will wrap it around your neck every time.

**What's the Last Word?**

Living with a tough child is tough, but every day try to do the following in some combination: Look your child in the eye, smile often, give a gentle touch, and say something pleasant. And unloving though they may be, see if you can tell them once a week that you do, in fact, love them. If you can't, don't worry about it. Some day you may be able to. You have plenty of time.

Oprah said, "Whatever you fear has no power. It's your fear that has the power."

P.A.C.T. says, learning P.A.C.T. strikes some as initially attempting to spin gold from straw, a process requiring courage to deal with the fear of a failing Spike. As rotten as he can be, Spike is still your kid and someone who needs a future with the least amount of misery possible.

Spike finds his game moderately more interesting than Angelique.

# Advanced Goal #14 : "That child gets under my skin like nobody else. He makes me so mad I could spit..."

## What's the Goal?

Don't let your buttons get pushed.

## What's in the Fine Print?

What are the three things your Spike can do to piss you off the quickest? Be rude? Ignore you? Act like he doesn't care? Attack other children in the family? Whine? Pester you until you scream? Follow you around the house saying, "But why? But why? But why? But why?" Think about this a minute. Think hard. List the things that you resent the most on a sheet of paper. After you have listed them, read them over carefully, and resolve never to react to them again.

Spike can now be as foul as he likes. He can be rude or degrading and it won't get so much as a whisker twitch out of you. Wouldn't you like to be immune to his nastiness? You can. It is in your power. All you must do is practice the stone face. Child says something rotten to you, and you give the child back nothing. Blank. No quiver. No emotion. No nothing. Show the child that what he does is beneath your notice by not noticing.

This is very powerful. After all, the reason for all the rudeness is its visible effect on you. So when your child calls you, "Fat Bitch!" in public you do what? Nothing. Why? Because it is effective. What will others think? They will admire your courage. Now, of course, if you do have an effective antidote handy, use it. Most parents in this situation don't. The key, however, is effectiveness.

This strategy is not because you like disrespect, or deserve it, or think it's healthy to have your child be foul. P.A.C.T. does not want you to be treated with contempt by your child. It wants your child to stop. He will if you are stronger than he is; not with the fight-fire-with-fire kind of phony strength. You will lose that contest. Rather, you are visibly stronger than any string of foul words he can put together. Your strength will inhibit its reoccurrence. The more Spike sees your strength, the sooner he will give up the assault. It is no fun to be crude to someone who is above it all. So, say nothing, do nothing. Gracefully leave the room and find something else to do.

We all have our buttons. Those closest to us know them better than anyone else. They know how to use them, too, and probably do anyway from time to time when they feel ornery. But we are talking about more than just occasional orneriness here. It takes a mean little child to trot them out for daily use. These, after all, are our private vulnerabilities. Feel sensitive about your weight? Spike will rub it in your face, preferably in public. Have a physical deformity? Have some personal failing? Spend the night with your boyfriend? None of them are safe with Spike. Spike wants to humiliate you with them. If they weren't humiliating he wouldn't bother. Using them against you borders on cruel. They are acid tests of your ability to be dignified. Any display of emotion is too much display.

If Spike can't torture you with these things, he can't torture you with anything. So, what do you do? List the three things Spike can do to irritate you the quickest. Resolve never to react. There may be more than three things he does but if you can triumph over these, you can triumph over the rest. This skill generalizes nicely.

## Is There an Alternative?

The easiest thing is to calmly get out and meander away. The harder thing is to stay and not budge. Make him be the one to leave. Concentrate on being peaceful. If your anxiety starts to rise, you are free to get up slowly and leave. Don't stay seated on the couch if it makes you nervous and you display it.

## What's the Last Word?

Living with a tough child is tough, but every day try to do the following in some combination: Look your child in the eye, smile often, give a gentle touch, and say something pleasant. And unloving though they may be, see if you can tell them once a week that you do, in fact, love them. If you can't, don't worry about it. Some day you may be able to. You have plenty of time.

# Advanced Goal #15 : "I Want It, and I Want It Now!"

## What's the Goal?
Don't sound demanding.

## What's in the Fine Print?

**Demanding is ordering someone around like a child, a child who lacks a brain.** Even children don't like being treated like children. It feels degrading or irritating. It feels as though someone believes you have no right to independent thought or action. It feels like someone believes they don't have to be polite because you are younger, weaker, smaller, or stupider than they are. Demanding is the essence of disrespect. When you complete this goal, you will relieve yourself of some of the frustration associated with making the futile gesture of demanding.

"Get over here!"
"Put that down!"
"Stop it!"
"I said no and I mean NO."
"I'll give you something to cry about, buster."

Several things are at work here while the parent is sounding demanding; all of them would be helped if Dad and Mom changed verbal tactics. Demanding speech contains levels of meaning. Most of them are unpleasant. All work against a parent who is attempting to work his or her way through P.A.C.T. As a communication style, demanding is more likely to encourage out-of-control behavior than not.

Demanding is rude. Since when is it the case that rudeness is an effective way to promote behavioral change? Some who intellectually understand this point know it is ineffective but continue to rely on it anyway. It is as if they say: "Hell, I know this is against everything I should be doing, but the little sonofabitch makes me so mad that it just, well, feels good to give him a taste of his own medicine from time to time."

Fair enough. It probably does feel good, if only for a moment. Parents must stop thinking that a child will respond to the insight that ought to occur when the child is treated as contemptuously as he treats others. Does it really make the child think twice about the way he talks to his folks?

Don't bet the rent money; demanding just builds more resentment. If parents put themselves in their child's shoes, they'd find the fit uncomfortable. All of a sudden, the issue would seem clear. Much of childhood misery is nothing more than taking adult anger and shoving it back at them.

First: Your child is a bit confused. He really does not understand all that is happening to him. He does not completely understand his anger or his oppositional behavior. As a result, he tends to target the people most important to him.

Second: If you ask the miserable child what is bothering him he won't tell you much. He does not know much on a conscious level. His anger is an attempt to cover up fear. It is more acceptable to show anger than fear, so he shows anger. His fear is rooted in his feelings that he is not worth much. He may be wrong, but this is what he believes. And he tries to proves it with his behavior. He does not act like a successful human being. He acts like someone who is failing. He does not know what his future will be but it will probably hurt. He is developing an "I don't care" attitude to give himself insulation from everything.

Third: He feels wrong, maybe even stupid. He also feels blamed. He is over-sensitive and imagines worse things than actually occur. He is defensive and easily threatened. As a result, he can be foul. He does not believe that he has the ability to make anything better. He also is none too sure that his life is his fault, in spite of the way he feels about himself. He is confused on this point. He certainly believes that life is not fair.

Fourth: He can't be talked out of these feelings. He doesn't trust talk. When he says to his parents, "LEAVE ME ALONE!" he really means it. To a large degree, P.A.C.T. does just that. It shifts the responsibility onto Spike's shoulders because he needs to learn how to handle it.

Giving up the impulse to parent is a tall order. Hardly anyone likes the idea. We all think we are entitled to demand compliance the way our parents did. Most of us can't imagine what good will come of abandoning attempts at traditional parenting. But everything we know about parenting is grounded in the assumption that we all have normal children. Not all of us do.

Rudeness will seriously undermine the process. It reinforces his negative feelings about himself. We want him to let go of those feelings and the behaviors that accompany them.

Demanding is angered. Anger directed at a miserable child will not produce the change the parents say that they want. Some parents act as if they want the ability to be angry more than they want their child's good behavior. If so, they will be reluctant to give it up. Those parents who are sitting on the fence trying to decide whether or not giving up their anger is a good thing should ask themselves what good things their anger brings them. It is doubtful whether there has been much. The reverse is more likely.

Demanding is arbitrary. The more unhappy your child, the more it may seem to him that everyone's dissatisfaction with him comes in spite of what trouble he actually causes. No one's dissatisfaction may seem connected to any particular sin. The child's feelings may be right. Children with a bad reputation are hassled the most. Teachers know these children. So do the police. As a result, either happiness or unhappiness directed to an already unhappy child seems arbitrary.

Maybe the child is confused in more ways than one; maybe he gets too much negative mixed in with the positive. It is common enough. A little negative can trump a whole lot of positive even among the happiest of us. He does not know what to believe so he believes the worst. We think he should differentiate the good from the bad. He can't. Since the child feels that he has little control over whether happiness occurs or not, he is inclined to give up and be consistently miserable.

Adult speech directed to this child contains many more negative messages than we may suppose. This child is used to extracting negative meaning. His over-sensitivity will find confirmation in the brusque and abrupt feeling of rejection he has had about himself as well as every feeling of resentment he has for people who speak to him this way. Once again, this is a contest of wills. We suppose that the unhappy member of the family will be more than willing to give up his unhappiness. Experience tells us that this will not happen. Adults must be the ones to lead the way. And they need to do so based upon some consistent logic.

Demanding is dictatorial. Giving orders, which is the essence of demanding, is ineffective. Not many children warm to having a drill instructor for a parent. Not many children like living in an environment in which everything seems to be either black or white. Drill instructors feel comfortable in black and white settings and hope to force children into the same setting. They can be forceful through strength of will, but it is unlikely that a child raised in such an inflexible environment can be expect to negotiate a flexible world. The drill instructor may live in a black and white world due to his own adjustment limitations but the world is neither accommodating nor forgiving of those who do not understand that the drill instructor is trying to force order on a disorderly world.

> He says his parents owe him. He has a black hole, somewhat smaller now, where his heart should be. His parents can't heal the hole. That's his job. All his parents can do is get out of the way. If he gets help, the hole will heal faster. He probably won't just yet. He will be cautious and conservative, yet sensitive and defensive.

Perhaps the greatest limitation to having a drill instructor for a parent is the likelihood that such a parent is insensitive to a child's emotional needs. The drill instructor is more interested in his perception of order and the illusion of discipline, than he is in listening. Such a parent may have a hard time drying tears or understanding anger. They won't have much tolerance for either.

## Is There an Alternative?

At least say, "Please" and make it sound as though you care. Don't make "Please" sound like one more demand. "PLEASE PASS THE BUTTER!" is a distortion of polite.

## What's the Last Word?

Living with a tough child is tough, but every day try to do the following in some combination: Look your child in the eye, smile often, give a gentle touch, and say something pleasant. And unloving though they may be, see if you can tell them once a week that you do, in fact, love them. If you can't, don't worry about it. Some day you may be able to. You have plenty of time.

Dale Carnegie said, "Today is the tomorrow you worried about yesterday."

P.A.C.T. says, worry is what most parents are reduced to as they have nothing else to fall back on. The evaporation of worry is a common secondary effect of P.A.C.T.

# Advanced Goal #16 : "You did it...I know you did it...just admit it!"

## What's the Goal?
Don't accuse.

## What's in the Fine Print?
**We accuse by using the word "YOU."** It is beyond commonplace. The word "YOU" has been used dozens of times in this book. It's easy. It's fast. Everyone knows what it means. Normally it is a fine old pronoun. But nothing is normal when it comes time to the miserable. "YOU" becomes a weapon, a target, an enemy. We say lots of terrible things with the word "YOU" in it:

"You are inadequate."
"You are a slob."
"You are stupid."
"You are a disappointment."
"You are bad."

"YOU" is often just not nice. Given the unpleasant things that we attach to the word "YOU," our goal is to eliminate use of the word. Parents find "YOU" the toughest goal, which is why it is presented later in the program. The toughness of this goal is a direct indicator of how important it is to everyone, even though they don't know it. Spike does not hear the word "YOU" in a benign, gentle context—things like "I love you" and "You're cute" —aren't part of his experience. "YOU" to Spike is all bad.

Eliminating the word means substituting something different in its place. P.A.C.T. is interested in taking things out of the parent's repertoire; in this case, we are going to substitute.

Here are examples:

"You clean your room."
"The room needs cleaning."
"Please clean up the room."

Doesn't look like rocket science, does it? It is, nonetheless, important. Like a number of other goals in this program, it may not look like much but:

1. Add up the number of times the miserable child hears the word "YOU" in the course of a day,
2. Analyze how people, including you, speak to the child

…and you will see that "YOU" is not a simple pronoun; it is a club.

The parent who removes the word removes accusation, blame, irritation, and all sorts of unhappiness directed to the child. By making the change, that is, de-emphasizing "YOU" and emphasizing the THING, parents give their child a message: "I am more interested in accomplishing some task than in making you squirm."

Open wide and say, "YOU." If a parent wants to show disapproval, he obviously can. If he does not want to, the task is tough. Those parents will invariably notice how much they use the word and how often its use can be interpreted negatively. This is, by the way, somewhat different than using "I" statements. "I" statements concentrate on removing the child as the topic, which is just fine. But removing "YOU" takes it a step further as it concentrates on eliminating accusation.

Spike and his kind feel attacked. This is why they are defensive. P.A.C.T. teaches you to cease the attack with the expectation that the defensiveness will likewise cease. "YOU" is a big part of their sensitivity. Spikes are attack-proof; that is, they will not respond well, they will not be intimidated, they will not give you want you want. It doesn't matter if they are guilty. Guilt is irrelevant. We assume they are guilty of something. But the issue is, how do you get past this step and onto the next with them? By acceptance.

> "YOU" is a powerful word. Every time Spike hears it, he assumes someone is blaming him for something. It is a reasonable fear. Someone probably is. He is as guilty as sin of something. But "YOU" has got to go. It just keeps him on edge.

## Is There an Alternative?

Eliminate opportunities to accuse. Be more careful of your things. Sure, you can leave your wallet, keys, watch and glasses out in plain sight. But maybe you shouldn't. Whenever one comes up missing, that is your clue that maybe you should have kept them under your pillow. Waking up in the morning and realizing that you have been had by your child should not trigger a round of accusation. It should trigger of round of resolve that you will be more careful in the future. After all, our impulse when he finds our keys missing for the umpteenth time is to say, " You took my keys again, didn't you, you little creep? I'm sick and tired of you stealing everything I own."

## What's the Last Word?

Living with a tough child is tough, but every day try to do the following in some combination: Look your child in the eye, smile, give a gentle touch, and say something pleasant. And unloving though they may be, see if you can tell them once a week that you do, in fact, love them. If you can't, don't worry about it. Some day you may be able to. You have plenty of time.

# Advanced Goal #17 : "Yes, you did. NO, I DIDN'T. Yes, you did. I DID NOT!"

## What's the Goal?
Don't argue.

## What's in the Fine Print?

Arguing with a miserable child is like participating in a match-up between weasels. First, it's one animal's turn, and then the other's. Soon you can't tell which is which. The hard part about arguing is understanding that you are vulnerable. Your child will trap you and exploit the weakness you expose. Arguing with them is weakness enough, which they understand perfectly, even though you don't. Adding such things as meanness or sarcasm is like adding sour milk to a cake mix: It just begs for trouble. Witness the following interchange between Mom and her little Spike:

"Can I have a dollar?" asks Spike.
"What for?" says Mom.
"For to buy something with, that's what for. Gimme the dollar."
"I don't have one."
"I know you do. Cough up."
"Go earn your own dollar."
"Like where can I get a job in 15 minutes?"
"You are so rude."
"Bite me."
"Go to your room!"
"Right! Are you gonna give me that dollar or do I have to get your purse myself? I shoulda done it already. Been a lot quicker."
"You stay out of my purse."
"What are you gonna do? Send me to my room?"
"Why don't you be nice once in a while?"
"Mommy please, can I have a dollar?"
"NO!"

"That's what I get for being nice!"
"Just go away."
"Gimme a dollar first."
"Then will you leave me alone?"
"Of course I will."

Mom gives him a dollar, and he goes away. Anybody looking at this argument can see many things immediately. In fact, the problems are so obvious that even Mom, bless her heart, will understand. We're not trying to be mean here: moms are distracted by a need to survive and may not see the forest for the trees.

- **First, the child knows that Mom will not stand her ground.** He can come at her from 12 different directions, including crudeness, and he will get his way.
- **Second, the child knows he can threaten and that the threats are intimidating.**
- Third, the child knows that if he pretends to be polite and it does not work, he is free to be obnoxious.
- **Fourth, the child knows that if he hangs in there long enough he will get wants.**
- **Fifth, the child knows that Mom feels guilty.**
- **Sixth, the child knows Mom has no control over him.**
- **Seventh, the child knows that Mom thinks she has struck some kind of bargain at the end but that is just for a little face-saving because he was going to win anyway.** Nothing has changed from the way he will act tomorrow…or after he comes back from spending the dollar.
- **Arguments with a difficult child are pointless.** Arguments must be choked off the moment they begin. The difficult child is stronger than the suffering parent. If you are incapable of changing a situation, don't try. You will just look foolish. If this means, for instance, your daughter walks out the front door looking like a slut, you may have to accept it knowing that you are essentially powerless to have her look otherwise. Better she walk out the front door without having won in a verbal battle with her parents.
- **Dump the argument:** If she walks out, she walks out…but not because you exposed your lack of control and thus, proved to her one more time how ineffective you are. Once you have done a good job of demonstrating self-control and non-confrontation, the behavior is likely to become more respectful.
- **Arguing is but one step in this graded approach. P.A.C.T. is like a box of chocolates, taking just the nut clusters and leaving the jellies.** The whole box must be eaten piece by piece. The power of P.A.C.T. lies in its cumulative effect. Here is another example of a fairly common interaction that goes nowhere. The father ends up looking silly which is the opposite of what he needs. The antidote lies in a parent's growing skill set, a skill set this father lacks.

> Arguments are silly. You will lose. Spike starts them with you intentionally; his intent is to lure you into quicksand where he can watch you drown.

"You're not going out looking like that," says Dad.

"What's the matter with how I look?" says daughter Felicity who looks like she is out for an evening on the street corner.

"You look cheap and no daughter of mine is gonna look cheap." he says back to her.

"This is the way my friends dress."

"Then your friends are sluts," he says, voice rising, veins on his neck bulging.

"Don't call my friends sluts! MA! Dad called my friends sluts."

"Leave me outta your fight." she says,

"MA!"

"All right, already so what do you want me to do?"

"Tell Dad…."

"She looks like a tramp," says Dad, "and she's not leaving this house and that's it period."

"I will."

"No you won't. And now you can go to your room."

"The hell I will."

"Don't talk to me like that you little shit."

"Oh, yeah…just try to stop me." (SLAM!)

"GET BACK HERE BEFORE I CALL THE COPS!"

- **Arguments are tailor-made for the weak.** What are the cops going to do, put her in jail? This parent is raising the ante and will lose. Daughter says, "GREAT!" She takes it as a challenge. She will learn that unless she does something worthy of arrest, the police have no interest in her. They have better things to do than chase an adolescent girl through town. Mom doesn't want to get involved because she knows this is a trap.
- **Parents have the impression that the police or judges or psychologists can do something that parent's can't.** They become embittered when they find it isn't true. The fact of the matter is, parenting the monster is inescapable. Most agents of change change little. The parent that places too much faith in a professional's abilities to create change will be disappointed. Perhaps the main function of the professional is to be supportive to parents. But parents want more. They assume more is out there. They are often wrong.

Rule of thumb: Say what you have to say briefly, don't repeat yourself and let whatever happens, happen knowing that some of it, at least initially, may not be pretty. Both of the conversations quoted here should have been cut off after the first few sentences or not begun in the first place.

## What's the Last Word?

Living with a tough child is tough, but every day try to do the following in some combination: Look your child in the eye, smile, give a gentle touch, and say something pleasant. And unloving though they may be, see if you can tell them once a week that you do, in fact, love them. If you can't, don't worry about it. Some day you may be able to. You have plenty of time.

Robert Byrne said, "Getting caught is the mother of invention." P.A.C.T. says, Spike doesn't bother to invent; he just lies. He really doesn't care if he gets caught or not. There is nothing you can do to him anyway and he knows it.

# Advanced Goal #18 : "He is so mean. And his father? Did I tell you about his father? Now there's a jerk!"

## What's the Goal?

Don't complain.

## What's in the Fine Print?

Here is the story of Martha, a wife and mother of three whose most obvious feature was her habitual complaining. Listening to a complainer is like listening to somebody tell bad jokes. It's excruciating. The urge to find the door is immediate.

- **Martha and her husband initiated P.A.C.T.** Their children seemed to have taken over the house, yelling and demanding. The oldest boy was 14. Two sisters were 10 and 8. The oldest boy had had a brief stay in a psychiatric hospital. One of the girls had a label of ADHD. The youngest child was, for the moment, label-free. The family's plate was full. It was basically a free-for-all. Martha didn't cope with it well.

> Complainers are tedious. No one cares. It's not as if a complainer wants change. They also want something to descend from heaven and deliver them. Complaining parents are weak and, therefore, despised.

- **Most families are reticent in front of strangers.** We'd need to be a fly on the wall to find out how most parents speak to their children, resolve difficulty, accept interruptions and set limits. If the fly in this family could talk, he'd say plenty. But, then, this family didn't hold back, so a fly wasn't necessary.
- **Martha's complaining might well be the thing that she did the best of anything in her life.** Over the first four weeks of this program she made virtually no progress. She complained that the children made her yell, and so yelling remained a major feature of her interactions with children. Her husband made progress, so he advanced to the next

level, while Martha stayed behind. Each week came with the same refrain, which went something like:

"They're still doing it."
"Doing what?"
"Driving me crazy"
"What are you doing about it?"
"What can I do?"
"The program."
"I want to, I really do, but the children are so awful."
"What do they do?"
"Bounce on the bed, leave dirty dishes around…"
"Is that all?"

> We say that we want Spike to change. But we do everything in our power to make sure he doesn't. For one thing, we can't get past the need to show him our disappointment by constantly complaining. In the meantime, Spike is struggling, but we can't see it.

"Isn't that enough? Well, maybe you'd forgotten but Frieda is ADHD, remember? And "Brian was in the psych hospital. He should go back, if you ask me."
"For doing what?"
"For driving me crazy. They won't listen. I just want to scream."
"What do you think the hospital can do?"
"Make them stop."
"Did they make him stop before?"
"For a few days, but it didn't last long. And they are the experts!"
"The child's behavior is not bad enough to need hospitalization. We shouldn't do that."
"What can I do?"
"Do the program. Change yourself. Do you still yell? Get angry? Call names? Threaten, criticize, and all the rest? You do, don't you?"
"Yes, but I don't have any choice and their pills don't help any."
"Did you make yourself a psych appointment?"
"I will. I just didn't get around to it yet. They'll probably tell me I need to take pills again, and I don't like taking them."

Martha has some serious problems. Complaining is only the tip of the iceberg. A behavioral program is unlikely to touch them in the short term.

- **First of all, Martha is stuck.** Her behavior suggests she will not extricate herself. Her antidote to her unhappiness is to complain. Her complaining is a plea for someone else to do what she cannot.
- **Secondly, Martha's family problems are not the real problems.** She demonizes her children when her real problem is herself. Most families referred to this program can get

a handle on their complaining very quickly. Martha cannot. Her husband continues to do well week after week. His efforts are undermined by his wife's inability to change.

- **Third, Martha was referred to other professionals on a suspicion of depression.** She went with reluctance. The threat of court intervention persuaded her to make appointments. Shortly thereafter, a complaint for suspected child abuse was made by the public school to the state. An investigation confirmed the report. She had lashed out at one of the children in public and was reported. And on still another occasion the school saw bruises, which were also reported.

- **Fourth, Martha has difficulty taking responsibility.** Problems are always someone else's fault, and usually the child's. Many parents feel as if the world is beating up on them, but they also have the ability to swallow hard, step back and do what needs to be done. Although this is a particularly difficult case, it is still likely to be at least marginally successful because of the presence of the father and, as it happens, the impending absence of the mother who will be permitted to visit on the weekends.

- **Martha clings to the possibility that the child's problems really are the child's responsibility and that they alone can solve them.** Her multi-year history with these is children should be evidence enough that they cannot and will not solve the problems themselves. Perhaps she is so vulnerable that she cannot tolerate any more of the lifetime of criticism that she has already received. Acknowledging responsibility seems like acknowledging guilt. She has guilt in spades already.

- **Fifth, note the relatively minor problems these people present.** In most families that use P.A.C.T., childhood behaviors are vastly worse: assaults, swearing, disrespect in public, fighting, lying, theft, fire-starting, assault, and all the rest. But that is not happening here. Her child's behavior could be, and perhaps in time, will be worse.

- **Not all parents who engage in chronic complaining have the same outcome as Martha.** Consider Elaine. She is remarried. Her estranged teenager came to live with her and her new husband because the boy's father died. Both mother and stepfather quickly learn to hate the child. The boy had a brief stay in a hospital before they began P.A.C.T. The following conversation is one Mom had with a neighbor who had been helping her learn P.A.C.T.

> "That child is such a puke. I just hate him."
> "What did he do this week?"
> "He is just at me continually. It's 'Mother this' and 'Mother that.' He eats like a pig, and his room is a disaster. I know he's stealing money, I just don't know from where. Not from us."
> "But you seem to be making progress. You don't yell as much. How about the anger stuff?"
> "I'm angry all the time, but I've just learned how not to show it. Showing it just makes things worse."
> "And criticism? How is criticism?"
> "He never hears any from me."

"Threats? Sarcasm? Tone of voice?"

"About a perfect as I can make them, but I'll get even better."

"Why the determination?"

"Because he is not going to ruin my life. I want this marriage to last, and the puke is not going to ruin it."

"How about not referring to him as a 'puke' anymore?"

"You are taking everything I hold dear away."

"I know. I'm mean. But how about it?"

"Okay."

"You mean it?"

"Absolutely. It doesn't give me that much satisfaction any more anyway. I'm even sick of complaining."

- **Elaine's disavowal of complaining is a good thing.** She was serious about getting rid of it. She is typical, although the problems her "little puke" displays aren't particularly serious. At least not yet. He is more like a case of Los Angeles smog during a cloud inversion: It lies over everything and threatens to choke out life, but life still goes on. When she first began the training, she felt as if her head were spinning. That stopped, and she just felt constantly exhausted. That stopped, too, and at this point she is just feeling a low-grade irritation. She confessed, almost sheepishly, at the last session that she might actually end up liking the boy, but that she shouldn't be quoted just yet.

Complaining tells us more than someone is disappointed. It seems to tell us that the complainer wants change. But change may be the last thing they have in mind. Complaining may exist for its own sake. It may seem sincere but it may be nothing more than the a pathetic display of ineffectiveness. Living with a chronic complainer is both a sign of depression and depressing to the person who must live with it. But it may also reveal itself over time as the symptom of someone who is just stuck in their own groove of misery, resistant to every attempt at change.

## Is There an Alternative?

If the point of complaining is to get support, there are better ways to get it. Consider enrolling in Al-Anon. It will be a good match to P.A.C.T. Consider Tough Love, too, if the problems just go on and on. There is a national organization called National Alliance of Mental Illness (NAMI) that has many chapters with parent support groups around the country.

## What's the Last Word?

Living with a tough child is tough, but every day try to do the following in some combination: Look your child in the eye, smile often, give a gentle touch, and say something pleasant. And unloving, though they may be, see if you can tell them once a week that you do, in fact, love them. If you can't, don't worry about it. Some day you may be able to. You have plenty of time.

Abraham Lincoln said, "Tact is the ability to describe to others how they see themselves."

P.A.C.T. recommends the golden rule in dealing with the Spike. It will confuse him at first, but he will come to appreciate it in time.

A peaceful car ride.

# Advanced Goal #19 : "You are a jerk, a loser, and a moron!"

**What's in the Fine Print?**
   If we would just confine ourselves to using everyone's given name, life might not be so bad for an unhappy child. But the urge to call Spike a puke is huge. Unhappy children work on our last nerves and tend to provoke nastiness as retaliation. When the heat's on, the names fly and they aren't pretty. Remember the nursery school rhyme your mother repeated to you, "Sticks and stones can break your bones but words will never hurt me."

- **Your mother lied**. Words can hurt badly. She knew it. You knew it. But you wanted to be comforted so you accepted the lie. Words are lethal. Consider, for instance: "You're FIRED!"
- **Those words are painful**. And it is a pain that takes a while to go away. Actually, what Mama was trying to get you to do was ignore bad things. What is the payoff in calling a child or anybody else: "a brat." "a jerk," "an asshole," "a little shit," or "a _____ !!!"
- **Nothing**. It will surely prompt less dignified titles. As the names get worse so, too, does the behavior. Why would any child, after being called "You little snot!" turn around and become tractable? It makes no sense. Unless, of course, the intention isn't change but rather just anger display. What does the parent get from all of this? A burst of immature self-satisfaction.

"Well, I guess I told him off, huh?" you say, boasting to yourself as though you had just won a boxing match. "Now he knows who is boss, the little shit."

- **Your child knows you think he's a snot or worse**. It isn't helpful. We know you get frustrated. We know that YOU know you shouldn't call names, but you do and, when you do your payoff is a little menace that is likely to be as bad as he has ever been. "At least," you say to yourself, "I got off a shot, so he knows how I feel."

- **Frankly, he has known how you felt for a long time.** He knows it isn't nice. So he digs in his heels and acts as though he doesn't care. But, he does. The end of a verbal cat fight isn't at hand just because you said something mean. Spike will play his card. It is doubtful that parents ever get in the last word when they are dealing with miserable children. Miserable children won't allow it. They just never seem to give up. When you tire of the menace sufficiently, you'll stop. When you stop, so will he.
- **The adult actually believes that the child may listen and stop.** But wishful thinking doesn't get anyone anywhere. Name-calling is a desperate effort to call attention to a child's shortcomings. The parent hopes it will be greeted with dismay and prompt change. It won't. Name-calling is part of a trap that parents create for themselves. The parent fools himself into believing that "If I tell him he is a jerk just one more time he'll stop."
- **He won't.** Such parents need another choice. It is a revelation when these parents find out that not engaging in name-calling is more efficient than engaging in names calling. Changing relationships in a conflict-ridden household does not require a new set of skills. Parents have the skills already. They just don't know it. And they won't know it until they submit themselves to the discipline of systematically removing from their behavior those habits that make life worse for everyone. This includes name-calling.

> Your task at all times is to be stronger than Spike. Not louder. Not meaner. Not arbitrary. Not thoughtless. Not impulsive. Stronger comes from within—it is reliable. It is ultimately loving. Name-calling doesn't fit in anywhere here.

The essence of name-calling is a lack of confidence parents have in themselves. There are few parents struggling under the unhappiness they share with their child, that need to struggle one day longer. Self-confidence flows from self-control.

## Is There an Alternative?

If you feel you have to say something, just say their name. Say it calmly. Take the emotion out of it. If you decide to say it more than once, use the saying of it to calm you down, as in GEORGE, GEORGE, GEORGE. Ol' George may wonder about you, but you didn't get carried away and say something that you will regret, so let him wonder.

## What's the Last Word?

Living with a tough child is tough, but every day try to do the following in some combination: Look your child in the eye, smile often, give a gentle touch, and say something pleasant. And unloving, though they may be, see if you can tell them once a week that you do, in fact, love them. If you can't, don't worry about it. Some day you may be able to. You have plenty of time.

# Advanced Goal #20 : "…and then I said, "Look Spike," and then he said something stupid, and then I told him again…"

**What's the Goal?**

Quit talking so much.

**What's in the Fine Print?**

We can hear you say to yourself: "Quit talking? So what am supposed to use—smoke signals?"

- **Yes, if you know how to make smoke signals, use them.** It is better than talking. For the rest of us, we have to mind the quality and quantity of our speech. Many parents of the miserable talk too much. You know the type. Maybe it's you. They go on and on. It is closely related to explaining or nagging. Maybe it is just a nervous attempt to fill dead air space.

- **There was the dad who had the following charge leveled against him by his wife: "Damn, Fred, but you are SO redundant."**

- **He was, too. It means he said the same thing all over again.** It was as if there were nothing in the child's life that shouldn't be repeated. This isn't nagging. It is just talky talk, over and over. This otherwise nice dad, in fact, had nothing new to say. Ever. He was a recycler of other's comments. You go out for coffee with this guy and his role was to repeat, reflect, or paraphrase what everyone else said.

- **You get the idea when you think of a bunch of retired farmers sitting in the Blue Bird Cafe all morning drinking coffee.** Somehow the weather is the mainstay of the entire conversation. They turn it over and over, upside down and back and forth trying to squeeze something new out of it.

- **Talking to Spike just to fill space is resented.** It suggests someone who feels they must be in control of the airwaves. The broader issue may be a controlling parent but the easiest way to access a controlling person may be through discouraging the things they attempt to control, such as the airwaves. They aren't going to get control over you any more that you will over them. It is up to you to recognize the problem and do something about it.

- **It bears knowing that this guy we've just described had several miserable children.** All of them just want to holler: "SHUT THE FUCK UP!"

- **Parental over-talk will encourage an otherwise nice all-American miserable child into rage.** He sees it as a form of torture and hates it. If this is your version of passive aggressive behavior, stop it. Its passivity will not be tolerated for long. Redundancy is at the heart of the parent who talks too much, not to mention insensitivity to the feelings of others or perhaps fear.

> Reasoning, by which we mean talking too much, is an invitation to be scorned. Face it: The sound of our voice is not pleasing to little Spike. He needs a period when he hears as little of it as possible. He needs to hear it only in specific, targeted ways and then not much. He will use this time to relax since he won't feel as threatened and, hence, as defensive.

"Maybe" she says to herself, "If I just say it one more time, he'll catch on and we'll all be one happy family again."

Are you crazy?

She is just as apt to say, "If I've told you once, I've told you a million times…"

- **This is the theme song of the hassled parent.** But only a million? She's an amateur. Quiz: What do you think is a consequence of having been told something a million times? Nothing. Nothing positive. It sure won't change anyone's behavior. Actually the parent is the only one being changed: parents get angrier and angrier. Your child will do nothing except ignore you and project his anger back on you, thus justifying his anger. This is not the outcome you want, presumably. But you may be stuck in a logic that goes something like this:

  (1) I am a reasonable adult and am well-behaved.
  (2) My son's behavior is unreasonable and poorly behaved.
  (3) Therefore, if I use reason with this unreasonable child, he will behave.

- **Fat chance.** Basing your campaign on talking on his unreasonableness is DOA. The assumption that his unreason will yield to your reason is naïve. Maybe in the abstract it may, but what if the unreasonable child holds you responsible for his unhappiness? Maybe this child does not find you reasonable. Maybe the only one who thinks you are reasonable is, well, you. Logic in order to be useful must be shared. Perpetual repetition is one-sided. If it is one-sided, it will be ineffective. If it is ineffective, no change is occurring. This is not a criticism of your efforts to be a good parent. It is an update of an old axiom that goes: She who lives in a glass house may as well give up and invite in the neighbors. Her vulnerability is more transparent than she thinks.

- **Your glass house is your vulnerability to talk, which comes from not understanding the basic give and take of relationships.** Unequal relationships do not work. That does not mean parental vs. child relationships should be democratic. It does mean that they should be mutually respectful. A mutual relationship is not one where just one person is doing the talking.

- **Part of this problem is coming to terms with parental ineffectiveness, accepting that ineffectiveness and moving forward.** You cannot deal with it if you don't understand it. So the next time your child screams at you in the supermarket and says, "SHUT UP!" take the hint. Summon your dignity and stifle. Identifying the problem need not have been a public event; you could have figured this out in the privacy of your own home.

- **In this case, ineffectiveness is demonstrated as too much talk.** Talk is almost always unnecessary. Aside from being redundant, it leaves you exposed. In the hands of the miserable, a talkative parent is a parent who is asking for trouble. Witness the screaming in the market. If the little so and so is not outright ignoring you, he is looking for an opportunity to destabilize you. He knows you are vulnerable. He doesn't know that your vulnerability is based on guilt:

"Well, I've got to explain to him so he'll know."

"He already knows."

"I mean what if he really doesn't know?"

"You've told him a million times already? Why wouldn't he know?"

"Maybe he wasn't listening."

"That's probably true, but it isn't the same thing."

"If I tell him just one more time, maybe he'll stop."

"And maybe the Ice Age will return."

"He is basically a good boy."

"Aren't they all?"

"You think I should say 'STOP' and let it go at that?"

"That's pretty much it."

Spike's parents are potential saviors. But their enabling can be infuriating; i.e., Mom says Spike refuses to talk to her. Fine. Life is peaceful without him. It won't last long anyway. But what does she do on his birthday? Gives him the same $100 she always gives. The message to the child? Spike can be a brat forever and still get $100. Mom is afraid he will think she's petty if she doesn't! So what? He can think what he likes. Mom says she knows best. She says, 'Maybe if I talk to him one more time…?' She doesn't completely believe that she needs to take her talk and sit quietly somewhere for a while.

"No more. THAT REALLY HURTS ME WHEN YOU DO THAT!"

"Not if it makes you vulnerable, not if his behavior isn't getting better. Save that sort of thing for a bit when things start to change around here, and he actually will act as though your feelings mean something to him. It will happen, but not just yet."

- **Being told to "SHUT UP" is crude and simply contributes to an already crude world.**

But, in this context, if it gets your attention it has done its work. So maybe we should just say: "S-h-h! Quiet" instead. That gets the point across, too. Say what you have to say to the child and stop. Give no more detail. The less, the better.

- Your verbal encounters should be brief and to the point, otherwise, he will find openings. The more you talk, the greater the opportunity that you will be manipulated. If he can push you into anger, he has won the exchange. If you can say what it is you have to say briefly and not be drawn into further conversation on the subject, you win.

- Perhaps putting this in terms of winning and losing seems too simplistic. The attempt to create a normal child out of an abnormal child is a battle. It has strategy. It has method. It should be clear in its goals. And it most definitely has losers—they are the children whose parents cannot, for whatever reason, create a safe environment so they can grow and have the luxury of liking themselves sufficiently to be successful.

- Successful lives require sacrifice. Unhappy children have little motivation to sacrifice. Life seems very unpromising to them. Their future life is likely to demonstrate it. If they are miserable, they are going to take you with them. Don't even think that sending them to, say, a residential school. You will just make them more insecure. If you do, you will find that the line from the horror movie: "HE'S BACK!" has more meaning than you dreamed. A therapeutic school may be a good idea, AFTER the parent has learned P.A.C.T. Put yourself on a diet to cut out the 25 pounds of hideous verbalization. It will only seem like a sacrifice for a little while.

**Is There An alternative?**

If you feel the need to talk a great deal about the child, there is always therapy available. You should be in therapy anyway just on general principles. If you need outlets because you are frustrated and you can get away from your children, affiliate with local charities. There are lots of them out there and they all need help. You can go on-line to find groups that struggle with the diagnosis your child has and join them. These have parents who have many of your experiences and may be helpful.

**What's the Last Word?**

Living with a tough child is tough, but every day try to do the following in some combination: Look your child in the eye, smile often, give a gentle touch, and say something pleasant. And unloving though they may be, see if you can tell them once a week that you do, in fact, love them. If you can't, don't worry about it. Some day you may be able to. You have plenty of time.

Russell Baker said,
"Don't try to make
children grow up to
be like you or they
may do it."

P.A.C.T. says, Spike's
behavior is more outrageous
than yours, but his behavior
still contains a hair of the
parent that is trying to
control him. Accept that
reality and model a whole
different kind of parent.
You will like it. So will he.

A quiet dinner with the family.

# Advanced Goal #21 : "Just where do you think you are going, young man?"

## What's the Goal?
Don't question.

## What's in the Fine Print?
Questions seem innocent. They aren't.

- **So here you are, the parent, in the car driving to the mall.** You don't much like malls but your wife wants to go and your teenage child, who generally thinks you should have the decency to appear in public with a bag over your head, has asked you to take him with you. You know it is going to cost you some money, but you like doing something for the little nipper once in a while. And this morning began well enough, that is, he hasn't done anything to irritate you yet. 'Course the day is young, but you put that out of your mind. You are experiencing a bolt of optimism without the justification to go with it. No matter. There is the illusion of the happy family in the family sedan, and your wife wants to strike up a conversation with Spike.

- **She should know that your child does not talk much.** She does. Boy, does she talk, and talk. That is one of her charms. She is good at dinner parties or family picnics because she can keep the conversation flowing. But this isn't a dinner party. This is a dysfunctional family. Your child normally spends his time being chased through town by the cops, drinking behind your house or anywhere else, skipping school, smoking marijuana, dropping acid, hanging out with the dregs, and staying out all night at God knows where. He is foul of tongue and lives in filth. But, for now, it is peaceable. You still have an intact family. You've often wondered how it is that you've managed to avoid divorce. You've prayed

> Much that we do in parenting these children is perceived by them as punishing and, thus, quickly rejected. It may not be what we intend, but it's what they understand. "Questioning" is one of many perceived attempts at punishment. It's not a good idea.

more than once that this child be removed. But now here you are, in the family car taking a family outing. You know this thing crackles with potential disaster. You hope everyone can control himself or herself.

- **Your wife gets the ball rolling.** She is starved for communication. She can't stand the tension and the family failure, so she asks:

> "So, how was school this week?"
> "I dunno."
> "Do you have a favorite teacher?"
> "No."
> "Oh, that's too bad. I always had one." (Silence)
> "Whatever happened to that nice boy, oh, what's his name…?"
> " Search me."
> "You remember, his parents live in that Colonial?"
> "Rick."
> "Yeah, Rick. He was such a nice boy. He never comes over anymore. Why don't you have him over?"
> "He's a moron."
> "Oh, I can't believe that. Call him up. We could make pizza."
> (Silence. He looks at his mother like she's an idiot.)
> "I'm sorry, but you could try harder, you know."
> "Ma!"
> "Can't I even help?"
> "Don't…just don't."
> "I JUST DON'T SEE WHY…."
> "OH, FUCK OFF!"

- **The exchange is typical of the out-of-control child.** Perhaps the only distinction between it and a real conversation is that it lasted as long as it did. Over-sensitivity and short fuses make for brief exchanges.
- **The culprits were the questions.** What are the dynamics in this exchange? First there is Mom. Bless her heart, all she wants is a normal child. So she is pretending. But school? Favorite subjects? They might be good as an icebreaker elsewhere. For a child who spends what few days he has at school serving in-school detentions, it's another matter. This child likely has no academic interests, nor has he a single teacher who can stand him.
- **If Mom wanted to enter this child's life at his level, she would have asked him what his favorite beer was or his preferred rolling papers.** In the absence of that kind of sincerity, Mom should not have tried. The result she got is the result she normally gets. She gets more anger and more crudeness. Is she afraid of silence? Maybe. If so, it is her undoing.
- **Moms like to question the socks off their children.** Mom is asking for trouble. She knows the child is not a conversationalist and nothing she does will make him one.
- **Mom thinks to herself: "If only I could get him to talk to me, things would be all right.**

If he'd just open up and let me know what is bothering him, then I could do something about it."

- **He is not going to open up.** He didn't open up to his shrink either. He just sat and stared at the ceiling. He thinks YOU are the problem, so why would explaining how he feels about you to you make a difference? He suspects it would not. He is probably right.
- **And while we are on the subject, here is a myth to dump: If I only knew what was troubling him, I could fix it.** Meaning, if he would just tell me what the problem is, I do could something about it. Really? You divorced his father, remember? How are you going to fix that? The guy was a serial two-timer; that's why you threw his stuff out on the lawn. The real problem here is that you can't abide the guilt that divorce could have caused all of this. Chances are it plays a role.
- **Questions are provocative as hell.** Mom's heart may be in the right place, but questioning is a self-control issue. Mom fears that silence equals rejection. It probably does. She mustn't find it threatening, however. Otherwise, she will undermine progress.
- **If the only way you can say something is through a question, don't say it.** Spike thinks he is being subjected to the Inquisition. Questions produce annoyance. Questions accomplish nothing. Questions are devices that seek to dump our need for conversation onto someone who can't deliver. And your response when he flips out is likely to be: "But I was just trying to…."

> We teach others how to treat us. Don't like the way Spike treats you? Teach him something different, but do it indirectly without resorting to questioning. Spike would rather suffer water torture than learn from you, so be clever. Think you can go toe-to-toe? Think again. Think you can outsmart him? Oh, yes. He is too absorbed in being a controlling menace to notice you are rebuilding yourself until you are actually rebuilt.

- **What…question?** We know what you were trying to do. But good intentions don't count here. The only things that count are those things that work. Constant inquiry does not make you a bad person, just one who creates more problems. So you say, "But I don't see why…."
- **If you still don't understand at this point, somebody needs to march you out behind the barn and shoot you.** You should understand the dynamics of the out-of-control child by now. If not, you are probably not going to understand something that involves you. Evidently it is too threatening. You are likely to say, "The doctor says my boy has a disease, and my neighbor says, 'Mercy, how you suffer,' and my ex-husband, now he's the real jerk in all of this, and the child, well, he's no prize either, I can tell you. So whaddya mean it's all my fault? I really resent that. If you knew how much I have had to put up with…"

You see? This mom doesn't wants the rap for producing a child like she got? Who would? The rest of us have learned to accept it, do what works and worry about understanding the problem after it goes away. It will actually be easier at that point than it is now anyway. Once you have cleaned up the junkyard of your relationship with your child, you can face some unpleasant truths and say to yourself: "I'm only human. I did my best. If I could, I'd have done better. If I had it to do over again, I'd do it differently. I gave the best I had at the time."

And you know what? All of that is true. Beware of the parent who looks perfect. There is a skeleton hanging in the closet of that perfection.

Can the questions. You do not need your child's confidence. You just think you do. You do not need to burrow inside your child and insist that he burrow inside you to make everyone whole. Normal children don't talk much to their parents anyway, so why would abnormal ones? Because they want your love and warmth, or you want their love and warmth so you can feel good about you? Good communication will occur naturally and spontaneously, not because you forced it.

## Is There an Alternative?

If what you want is information, then find someone else to get it for you, maybe a sibling whom your unhappy child trusts or someone outside the family. If it is conversation that you seek, then you will have to go without.

## What's the Last Word?

Living with a tough child is tough, but every day try to do the following in some combination: Look your child in the eye, smile often, give a gentle touch, and say something pleasant. And unloving, though they may be, see if you can tell them once a week that you do, in fact, love them. If you can't, don't worry about it. Some day you may be able to. You have plenty of time.

# Advanced Goal #22 : "I can't deal with it. I'm tired, frazzled, and don't know what to do."

## What's the Goal?
**Don't appear frustrated.**

## What's in the Fine Print?
**Poor frustration control speaks to your lack of patience and confidence in yourself.** But still you say to yourself: "Right, no visible frustration. And when do I get to be normal?"

Not for a while, certainly not now. You can't afford it. So get your chin up and stay focused. A continuing theme in this odyssey is your child's over-sensitivity. Over-sensitivity is a bit like being gun-shy; you know when the trigger is pulled there is going to be a big bang. You flinch in anticipation of the bang. Miserable children, while they are confused about many things, understand that they are inadequate. They anticipate rejection. A display of your frustration is just one more insult.

- **Frustration is the complement to tone of voice.** In tone you say it; in frustration you show it. Most of us have a hard time hiding how we feel.
- **Frustration is a vulnerability we have that we don't need.** It is a message to us that we are allowing something to bother us. Most things we feel frustrated over are trivial, as in: "SHUT THE GODDAMNED DOOR!"

A sense of frustration is a big signal. We can pay attention to the signal and do something smart or we can be self-indulgent and say, "He just made me SO frustrated...!"

- **Big deal.** This statement is just a bid for sympathy and self-sympathy from anybody around us who is willing to give us a little. A little support now and again is not a bad thing but a bid for support that says, in effect: "This burden is too heavy. You take it."

This is nothing more than an attempt to slide out from a job that cannot be filled by anyone else but you. Don't give into the temptation. There are few things more rewarding than self-control. It is the antidote to the pressure you generate for yourself, and an antidote to the terrors visited upon you by the miserable.

### Is There an Alternative?

Quickly find something positive to get your head into. Maybe it has something to do with the child, maybe not. Maybe there is something in the room (certainly not your child) that gives you some pleasure when you contemplate it. Focus on that for a bit.

### What's the Last Word?

Living with a tough child is tough, but every day try to do the following in some combination: Look your child in the eye, smile often, give a gentle touch, and say something pleasant. And unloving, though they may be, see if you can tell them once a week that you do, in fact, love them. If you can't, don't worry about it. Some day you may be able to. You have plenty of time.

Ralph Waldo Emerson said, "Nothing can bring you peace but yourself."

P.A.C.T. says, You can't make Spike happy. But you can create the conditions where he is likely to do so for himself.

# Advanced Goal #23 : "I really like that bolo tie."

## What's the Goal?

Don't initiate conversation.

## What's in the Fine Print?

**Conversation is for equals or at least for people on the same page.** Ever notice how much your child doesn't want to talk to you? Just because you wake up optimistically one morning and want to take one more stab at creating a relationship does not create an obligation in him. Your efforts to get him to accept that obligation are doomed. You know this is true because you say something like: "Good Morning!" And he says, "Stuff it." So you say, "C'mon, it's a nice day. Let's get along." And he says, "Get outta my face." Hopefully, you have learned not to say anything because you can see where this is going.

- **This goal encourages the parent of an actively miserable child not to initiate conversation until it is safe to do so.** This does not mean we want this child to get a sense of rejection. You are free to drop in a one-word something or other once in a while just to let the child know you are still here, you love him, and that he has not chased you away. But it's not going to be anything more substantial than that. "Hi!"

This is not a question. It asks little or nothing from him. This carries with it minimal threat and, thus, minimal need for his verbal defensiveness. You're not giving him any particular opportunity to come back at you. Of course, he can be unpleasant any time he likes, but you are not setting him up. Don't expect a response. If you get one, don't expect it will be charming. Say it for its own sake. Then drop it.

- **In practice, what this goal does is place the responsibility for generating conversation onto him.** It is much more likely that when you do this, you will get a much nicer comment from his mouth that you would otherwise.

- **Not initiating conversation frees the parent from the responsibility of having to be cheerful.** They no longer have the responsibility for the emotional tone of the family. Now they are freed to concentrate on other things.
- **Not initiating conversation is like having a weight taken from the shoulders.** You know the child is probably itching for a fight. You are just making it harder for him to start one. You now understand his tricks better than he does. You've heard about reverse psychology? You are doing just the opposite of what the child expects.
- **Like other goals, this goal will not fit well at first.** It will seem odd, uncomfortable.

"I am the parent," you say to yourself. "I am supposed to be the nice one. I am supposed to keep trying to make things better."

We crave a kind word from our Spike and often begin anew in an attempt to get it. But he uses any occasion to be rude. He takes our impulses and wipes his feet on them. He actually has a lot he'd like to say and not all of it's nasty. But the more you initiate, the less you'll get. It's a matter of trust that there is more going on in that heart of his than either of you can see. The antidote is simple: Be patient.

Of course you are. But when the role is thwarted, then what? Do you press on in the face of resistance? Not if you want change you don't

- **How do you know when enough is enough?** You experiment. You will not go through life avoiding conversation with your child. You can stop when he allows you to. How will you know when that is? You experiment. Ask him an occasional question. If his response is polite, maybe you can think about doing it again soon. If it isn't polite, then obviously he is not ready for a normal exchange, so you hold back. You wouldn't take a cake out of the oven before it is ready but you would look in the window to see if it is done. There is no point in rushing on either score.

If you stop to think about it, conversation initiation is the most obvious goal to illustrate what P.A.C.T. is all about. Parents may experience relatively long gaps in conversation but when they occur, they will be initiated by the child and will be more polite. Those long gaps are okay. Don't worry about silence. It's your friend. You've got the rest of your life to communicate. You are setting the stage. Your child appreciates the quiet. Just remember there is a difference between silence and the silent treatment. This program is not selling rejection. The occasional non-directive "Hi" will suffice until he is ready to make it more.

**What's the Last Word?**

Living with a tough child is tough, but every day try to do the following in some combination: Look your child in the eye, smile often, give a gentle touch, and say something pleasant. And unloving, though they may be, see if you can tell them once a week that you do, in fact, love them. If you can't, don't worry about it. Some day you may be able to. You have plenty of time.

# Advanced Goal #24 : "Well, I remember you beat up that nice boy last year, so I can't trust you…"

## What's the Goal?
Don't dredge up the past.

## What's in the Fine Print?
Dredging may be okay for shipping canals but it is hell when applied to a child by a parent who says they want change. It contains a message: "I know you are a jerk because you've always been a jerk."

The best predictor of tomorrow is yesterday. But, on the other hand, if you don't act like you have confidence in the child, why on earth should he? If you have to lie like crazy by omission and can do so with a straight face, do it. Honesty is for those who can afford to hear it. No matter how real his jerkdom is, you need to sidestep reminding him.

- **Dredging up the dirt relies on one-sided memories.** One of the most important distinctions between us and other life forms is our super memory. It means we can store experiences and can draw upon them again. If we could not rely on our experiences we would need to reinvent the accomplishments of others and of ourselves as well. Everyday we'd have to figure out how to make a fire all over again.

However, like all good things, this one has a dark side. We tend to make use of the dark side when dealing with the miserable child.

- **We have perfectly good understanding of how this child responds.** We've seen it before. We'll see it again. That information tells us a lot about how we should react. There is a difference between memory and experience. The former is like an empty ice cube tray. The latter is the cold water we put in it. What we experience, we stick in memory and store for a long time. Dogs remember who hit them. Elephants do too. No reason children wouldn't remember and dislike it when others rub their noses in it. We need to forget about some of the cold water we are making into ice. It's not helpful and takes up space.

- **Enjoy having your sins trotted out in front of you?** No one, child or not, likes to be reminded of his miserable past even when he deserves it. Our child's past—his habits, his predispositions and longings—are stuff for our memory but that is where they should stay. The good news is that we can change our perception with time and effort. The better news is that as the parent gets good at P.A.C.T., they become selective about what they wish to remember.

- **The child is used to feeling lousy.** He knows he is a child of few accomplishments, he hangs out with scrufties, and doesn't live up to any kind of potential. He knows a number of things about himself, and most of them are negative. The last thing that is likely to be a useful motivator is to remind him of his failings. They are a demonstration that we have no more confidence in him than he has in himself. And while that may be perfectly true, it is a mistake to let him know it.

> We feel a rush of superiority when we remind our deficient child about what a pain he was last week, and the week before that. Reminding him what a disappointment he has always been to us can only engender hatred.

- **Dredging up the past has little to do with the future, which is where we need to be.** His past governs our judgment but at the same time we need to keep quiet about it. Keeping quiet has its own charms. It is a statement about our willingness to put our child's needs first and our needs second. Parents often feel as though they have been putting their child first forever. They haven't. It just seems that way. Our Spike has been so insistent in his misery that he has taken over. Willingness to take, even temporarily, a secondary role is essential to turning the child around. It is not a role that should be permanent. Parents should come first because it is up to them to guide the way for their children. It is hard to be first when you are sitting in the back of the bus. By intentionally placing ourselves second, we are assuming the control that we can take subsequently.

So we are resolved to avoid the statement: "You always…." because even though he may always, he sure does not want to hear about it and will let us know in his own special way, as in: "DROP DEAD!" which accomplishes nothing. Spike has one more opportunity to be disrespectful. It is not good for him. Goodness knows it is hard on us. A child cannot value what he has not learned to accept. The value of learning to accept parental discipline is an important childhood experience that maps directly onto adulthood.

- **Dredging up one's past is a real downer.** Some things are better forgotten. We need to give Spike reasons to move on, not backward. Disrespecting one's parents becomes disrespecting one's supervisors. Spike may assume that if he can continually stick it up his parent's nose, then he can do the same at work.

Respect means boundaries. They may seem arbitrary. They aren't. The insecure parent has a tough time understanding his own sense of boundary and thus has a hard time communicating what this child's boundaries are as well. The hypersensitive child, who already has learned very little about respect and boundaries, can be counted on to learn even less if his vulnerabilities are prickly. The caring parent, therefore, will be aware that a history of failure is not a good platform from which to stimulate change.

## Is There an Alternative?

He may or may not be at the point where you can say something positive and have him respond well. If not, postpone. If so, find something positive, make a fleeting mention of it and move on. He is also sensitive to parents or teachers who exaggerate whatever he does because they think it is good for him. Praise will be seen for exactly what it is: nonsense.

## What's the Last Word?

Living with a tough child is tough, but every day try to do the following in some combination: Look your child in the eye, smile often, give a gentle touch, and say something pleasant. And unloving, though they may be, see if you can tell them once a week that you do, in fact, love them. If you can't, don't worry about it. Some day you may be able to. You have plenty of time.

Thomas Fuller said that, "He who fears your presence, will hate your absence."

P.A.C.T. says, Spike who seems to revile you to your face, will initially resent that he can't control you anymore as you learn to step away from the snares he sets for you. The more you step away, the greater he will accommodate your absence with kindness and respect.

# Advanced Goal #25 : "But the reason why I said it was…"

## What's the Goal?
Don't explain yourself.

## What's in the Fine Print?
Miserable children (1) generally know right from wrong; (2) generally assume that their parents think they do not understand a thing; and (3) manipulate the difference. As a result, parents figure they need to explain themselves to this-dumb-as-a-log child. Don't fall for it. Too often in the dark recesses of the parental mind, a guilt-ridden voice calls out, "How dare you value yourself so highly that you don't need to explain yourself. Who do you think you are? Somebody important? Go to your room."

- It says more about parental weakness than it does about a child.
- **Parents have learned to limit their vulnerability to their child's manipulation.** One way this is achieved is to limit the amount of verbal material we offer them—what we don't say, we don't have to regret. There is a tendency, huge in some and less substantial in others, to try to talk an unhappy child into cooperation. This is notorious for its failure rate, and parents know it. When interviewed, parents inevitably say that they, in fact, know that they talk too much.
- **Explaining goes to our needs, not Spikes.** The parent of the unhappy child figures that the child just does not understand; that the reason this child is so foul is that no one has taken the time to explain to him just what it is that people find so intolerable. This is the impulse behind sending children to therapists. Maybe, they think, a counselor can straighten the child out since the parent clearly failed. Thus, the parent concludes is that all someone needs to do is to explain the situation. The little nipper, being the bright lad that he is, will understand and, hence, adjust his behavior accordingly. That would be if it were true.
- **Explaining comes to us out of a theory.** One of the unjustified assumptions that civilians

have about counseling is that if a client understands why he feels the way he does, then things will be better. But if all it took was mere understanding, we could do counseling by e-mail. Understanding is only a start. Similarly, explaining tries to achieve the same end and it also does not work. Explaining may even make things worse as it is resented.

- **We assume that if a miserable child wants an explanation he will give the appropriate signals.** Will the child make a mistake while he is making up his mind whether to ask a parent or not? Probably. But life comes with consequences The consequences of making a mistake are something that children need. Is it tough to watch your child make errors? Sure, but considering how difficult he has been to live with and how many errors he has made so far, watching more of his mistakes is not a difficulty that should give anyone pause. Been there. Done that. Move on.

The reason for this is purely pragmatic: The child is not going to listen anyway. You cannot save him from error because he does not wish to be saved by you, or maybe by anyone else. Will his error make him an instant convert to the kind of child you would like to have? Probably not, but you are making him responsible for the outcomes of his own actions by not giving him reasons to dismiss you. Time will do the rest.

### Is There an Alternative?

Take a 3 x 5 card and write something on it, such as "Because I said so" or "The Answer is no." These may keep you from the temptation to embroider with an explanation which turns into a trap. Language is your enemy. Say nothing. Flash one or the other of these cards, remain silent, wait for a protest, and flash the card again. If you are good about this, your child is likely to stop. He is angling as hard as he can to get you to say something. He always could in the past.

### What's the Last Word?

Living with a tough child is tough, but every day try to do the following in some combination: Look your child in the eye, smile often, give a gentle touch, and say something pleasant. If you can't, don't worry about it. Some day you may be able to. You have plenty of time.

# Advanced Goal #26 : "NO, Impossible, Can't be done, out of the question…"

## What's the Goal?

**Don't be negative.**

## What's in the Fine Print?

**We can't be negative without someone to share it with.** We are all used to the child who has a perpetual snarl on his lips, who can't seem to say a kind thing to anyone and who is itching for a fight. The child may have his parallel in one (or both) parents. The child who has a chip on his shoulder may be the child who has a parent with a similar chip. If his life is just one big challenge to the world to knock that chip off, maybe he is modeling something.

- **How can you tell?** Try putting yourself on a diet of never using the negative, always forcing yourself to express things in the positive. For some, this will be easy. For others, it is a life-altering challenge.
- **Negativity can be a way of life.** It can become so habit-forming that it seems a part of life.
- **A negative child is grouchy.** He sees the world as half-empty rather than half-full. He can't bring himself to see the bright side of events.
- **Want an example of institutionalized negativity?** Listen to the local news. First, if it bleeds, it leads. Second, seen any weather reports recently? If there is a hint that the day will be anything less than perfect, the hand wringing begins. How do they report the prospect of rain? Unless it is a report in western Kansas, which hasn't seen rain in months, the report is negative. Rain

> Are you a glass half-empty or half-full type? Knowing makes a difference. We like optimistic people. They are half-full types. They look on the bright side. They are accepting. They deal well with disappointment. They accept responsibility for error. They know boundaries. They can have a miserable child, but they show the way out of the fog better than their counterparts. It's all about attitude.

represents some unhappy departure from the perfect cloudless day we are all apparently entitled to have. In fact, people who have gardens look forward to free irrigation.

- **For the sake of learning this step, the parent must find nothing wrong with anything.** He or she can only see the up side of life. Anything that might be down must be expressed as up. We want to see the silver lining.
- **The old statement is appropriate: "If you can't find something nice to say, don't say anything at all."** To that we can add: "but just try."
- Your obligation is to consistently find the nice. You may say, "Well, isn't this kind of phony? After all, there is misery out in the world."
- **Of course.** But, for the sake of learning a new interactional style, you need to act as if even the awful has its merits. Practice the reverse. Are you a battle-hardened Republican? Try smelling the Democratic daisies or help your neighbor wash his Volvo. Or, were you born with Birkenstocks? Trade them in for wing-tips and a flag pin for your lapel. Do it all with a smile.
- **The practice that comes from repeatedly seeing the upbeat will be refreshing and down right Socratic.** You will be relieved from the obligation of feeling crushed under the weight of a child's unhappiness. You have the power to lift yourself up or keep yourself unhappy.
- **Negativity should be no more intrusive on your Spike than any other goal.** A child who wakes up to a mother or father who has suddenly become transformed into Rebecca (or Fred) of Sunnybrook Farm may find the experience revolting. The intention is not to be in this child's face with a Cheshire cat smile from morning to night. The intention is, without fanfare, to change yourself so that the child may follow.
- **This goal is one of the few that does not ask the parent to simply remove a bad habit.** It is fairly easy, once the offending habit becomes conscious, to change it into something positive. So, that is what we will work on. Still, for the sake of record keeping, parents are asked to note the number of negative statements they make. For the sake of ease, a negative statement will be any statement that contains the words: "NO," "NOT," "NEVER," or "NOPE." You get the idea. "NO, you can't smoke that joint in my house" becomes "Joint smoking goes outside."
- **What happens here?** You take the emphasis off the negation and place it on the object. You end up saying what is important. Put the subject first. Here is another example: "You can't go to the dance and that's final" becomes "We'll try the next dance in February."

> Dishonesty is a terrible thing. Yes, for a while you have to be careful about what you say and how you say it. Saying less is often saying more. Still, throughout the process Spike must rely on what you say. You may not say everything you think and feel. We hope you don't. But, what you do say must be truthful. Playing games with the truth will bite you hard. You can't completely hide how you feel, but the better you control things like negativity, the easier it will be on Spike. Tact trumps honesty any day.

Actually, negativity is an attitude more than it is a presence of a specific word. Appearing optimistic, upbeat, helpful, and happy will probably have the desired effect. It requires thinking ahead and strategizing until such time as it becomes automatic. Being around a positive person is a joy and it is hard to dislike. They just continually see the best in others, find something upbeat and positive about everything, compliment others, ask about their families, their day, and take the time to listen. Take the time to seem interested. When someone calls you on the phone, spend the first few minutes asking about them. Don't let negative personalities drag you down. You will begin to notice them and wonder if you sounded just like they do.

## Is There an Alternative?

Every time you hear yourself saying "NO" in one of its many forms, stop and take a moment to think. It may have been entirely appropriate. After all, your child hasn't heard the word much. But it may also be a symptom of a desperate attempt to control. P.A.C.T. does not advise going back on what you said but maybe the next time the subject comes up, you can be prepared for it and seem more positive. There will always be a next time. Another test: Listen to yourself answer the phone. Is it upbeat? No? Practice sounding optimistic. This has everything to do with attitude.

## What's the Last Word?

Living with a tough child is tough, but every day try to do the following in some combination: Look your child in the eye, smile often, give a gentle touch, and say something pleasant. And unloving, though they may be, see if you can tell them once a week that you do, in fact, love them. If you can't, don't worry about it. Some day you may be able to. You have plenty of time.

Cordell Hull said,
"Never insult an
alligator until after you
have crossed the river."

P.A.C.T. says, telling
Spike he is grounded
when you can't enforce
it is asking him to
eat you alive. He will
happily do it.

# Advanced Goal #27 : "Who me? Drag my feet? Nonsense. I'd love to help you."

**What's the Goal?**
Don't be passive-aggressive.

## What's in the Fine Print?

**Passive-aggressive behavior is masked behavior.** Each of us tries to hide our limitations from the world in the hope that our smiles will be misread as happiness or our anger as strength. Both the smile and the anger may be attempts to cover our fear. Or they may be a game. For example, Spike hates planning. Parents plan in order to make families work. But Spike doesn't think beyond the moment. Some of that reluctance is passive aggressiveness. It is resistance. A child's foot-dragging smacks up against a parent's need to plan. A husband's foot-dragging collides with his need to take out the trash per the wife's direction.

- **Passive-aggressive behavior is aggressive behavior which is performed passively.** We expect aggressive behavior to be, well, aggressive. But how about the situation where the boss or the parent is much more powerful than you? Or someone wants to be devious? How about the situation where you have some resentment and feel like you need to display it but are afraid to do so directly? Or where you just like to subtly torture? In these events, you are likely indirect.
- **Passive-aggressive behavior is subtlety undermining and negative, but can pose as helpful concern.** It is like a toothless smile (the lips part, but decayed teeth are exposed). It is akin to lying; it is throwing a monkey wrench into a set of gears and saying, "Me? You've got to be kidding? Why would I do a thing like that? I love my job. It was someone else who erased all the files. And what's more, it hurts me that you think I'd do such at thing."

An investigation finds his fingerprints all over the thing. In fact, he probably hates his job but can't admit it. He doesn't have another one to go to. If he did, his behavior would be quite different. Passive-aggression is the friend who comes to your house and cannot say anything positive but, rather, manages to constantly finds fault. It may be the wife who subtly refuses, through foot dragging, to put in a load of her husband's laundry because it's a betrayal of her resentment of his crappy attitude. The refusal to do the laundry or to do the laundry badly is not an in-your-face refusal. That could be too scary. In some settings, you might get hit. It is just something that never gets done or gets done poorly in spite of all the nagging. Or maybe she puts in too much bleach or she washes on cold so they look dingy. It is a failure to get the job done for any number of reasons, all of which are a little bit bogus but not outright lies. Maybe she says she couldn't get to the laundry because:

(1) She was paying bills.
(2) Spike asked me to play a game.
(3) She was out all afternoon giving blood.

The most important point: the job gets postponed just as long as possible due to excuses. The intent is (1) not to do the job, and (2) to manipulate someone into anger while the perpetrator stands back in mock and saddened surprise.

- **Passive-aggressive behavior is very difficult to see and thus, a hard sin to ferret out.** The problem? It is about as easy to detect as oxygen and just as widespread. We all engage in it whether we understand the concept or not. It is something like guerrilla warfare: people shoot at you from behind rocks, but you can't see a thing. Blood is pouring out of your chest, but you can't figure out why. You doubt yourself, saying: "Nah, this can't be right. It's all in my mind. I just think I'm bleeding to death." And then, BLAM!

It takes a lot of bullet holes to convince you aren't crazy. The technique mastered by some adults is subtle but effective. Why should anyone want to attack from a distance? Fear! Fun! The victim knows that if they see the perpetrator hurling a rock or an insult at them, they could, in return, beat the living daylights out of them. People are passive-aggressive against a foe who is bigger, meaner, and more threatening than they. And because the foe is these things, in the mind of the victim, the foe is slow to catch on. It's a way for the weak to even the score. In this situation, the perpetrator is more likely to be the parent. Spike is stronger, at least initially, and doesn't have much need to be passive-aggressive.

- **Passive-aggression is devious and anonymous.** The recipient of the aggression can't believe anyone could actually assault him and get away with it. But the perpetrator often does. Let's say Dad gets a phone call and Mom doesn't tell him, and furthermore denies that the phone call was ever received. When confronted later by Dad, Mom says that she is sorry but it must have slipped her mind. It's indirect revenge. It's dishonest.

Here is another example:

You go to a party. Everyone arrives. There are the usual hugs. One of the guests tells you that your tie is dirty. Why did he do that? It was just out of the blue. It wasn't as though everyone was sitting around talking about how often they drool. He just came up to you and said, "There's a spot on your tie." So you go find the washroom and clean it as best you can. Did he intend that he would be helpful or was the intention to be annoying? Or to embarrass you? Does this person tend to do this sort of thing? In this case, the answer to all three questions is yes. It was passive-aggressive. How do you know? Because this isn't the first time he has pulled something like this. He was attempting to annoy you, as he has in the past and it worked because he resents you and his ability to annoy you is about the only power he has over you. So how did you react? Just exactly the way he wanted.

Now, had you been wise, you'd have ignored him. Why didn't you? Cause he gets under your skin. You basically don't like him. He knows it. You know it. When you are around him, you do your best to be pleasant but it is often an effort cause this guy is just plain annoying. Problem is, of course, you like everyone else in the group so you are, at least for the moment, stuck.

- **Irritation is a way we know that someone is manipulating us.** If we find that someone is getting under our skin, yet we examine what that someone is doing and it seems mild, maybe we are being subtlety tortured. It's like the friend who is habitually late. Or the spouse who won't come to supper without being asked three times and the last at the top of your lungs (not that you do that any more, of course). Just because someone is passive-aggressive does not also mean that he can't be aggressive, too. The truly clever are flexible in their approach to you. Those who are directly aggressive do not rely on passive-aggression a lot because they don't need to. They just come right out and whack us. But being passive-aggressive has its own charms, so why not indulge once in a while. Also maybe someone else in the family is stepping up. Or maybe things in the household have calmed down, but they aren't perfect. Maybe somebody still feels he needs to fight back. Maybe that somebody is us.
- **Not all noncompliance is passive-aggressive.** One important criterion is its effect on the victim. The victim is less likely to feel angry than he is to feel initially confused. He may well suspect something but he is likely to give you the benefit of the strength until he knows better. Strong people are more susceptible to this kind of manipulation. Their supposed strength blinds them to their exposure. People who are convinced that they are perfect are the passive-aggressors' victims. These parents won't catch on for a long time. They can not imagine—or have the self confidence to admit—that anyone could have discretion over them.
- **Someone who wants to counteract passive-aggressive behavior in another cannot afford to accept much at face value.** "You say, the wood didn't get chopped because of your need to pay bills? Okay, mind if I take a look at the checkbook?"
- **We remain calm when calling someone's bluff.** Passive-aggressive behavior can be aggravating, which, after all, is the intention. In repairing one's own relationship with someone, we can't resort to passive-aggressive behavior for the sake of revenge. The impulse should be avoided. Nothing good will come of it. The easiest way to see this kind of behavior in anyone else is to see if we can notice it in ourselves. The key is, "How many times this week was your behavior toward this person dishonest because you felt a twinge of resentment and wanted a slice of delicious revenge?" Did you set the cold milk out on

the counter to get warm? Did you place his breakfast in a place the cat could get it? Did you say you'd do something, but didn't?

- **We mentioned earlier that honesty is not the best policy with a difficult child. That** continues to be true but it is a goal. What we don't want as a substitute is dishonesty. In between lies tact. P.A.C.T. is all about projecting yourself in a consistent, stable, supportive and accepting way. You can't do it by becoming the jerk you say you don't want your child to be.

Passive-aggressiveness can be expressed in numerous ways:

1. Pretending not to understand something, thus compelling the person to repeat themselves
2. Avoiding responsibility
3. Forgetting
4. Lateness
5. Complaining
6. Lying
7. Intentional inefficiency
8. Losing things
9. Stubbornness
10. Obstruction

These are all easier to see in others than in ourselves. So the first step might be to concentrate on those persons with whom you are the least comfortable. See what you can detect. Then look in a mirror. You may be doing the same thing. The question of the day is, how many times was I devious today for the sake of driving my child (or anyone else) nuts?

## Is There an Alternative?

Honesty. Say what you mean, mean what you say. Forget the ambiguity. Do what is expected of you thoroughly.

## What's the Last Word?

Living with a tough child is tough, but every day try to do the following in some combination: Look your child in the eye, smile often, give a gentle touch, and say something pleasant. And unloving, though they may be, see if you can tell them once a week that you do, in fact, love them. If you can't, don't worry about it. Some day you may be able to. You have plenty of time.

# Advanced Goal #28 : "Well, I shouldn't let you out the door, but just this once…"

## What's the Goal?

Don't waffle.

## What's in the Fine Print?

**You've been through a lot of self-discipline by now.** One goal tends to slip over onto the next constructing a seamless and automatic detachment from your child's unhappiness. You may feel like you can be more spontaneous or that you can relax your standards or that you can cut your child some slack from time to time. Be careful. He needs your consistency. He needs to know that there are boundaries he can rely on. Do not be a softee. Be kind but clear. In spite of what he says, he wants the boundary.

- **Consistency is all about stability.** No hedging. No tip-toeing. Being predictable. Being as transparent as possible. Discretion still matters. It is an acknowledgement that by this point your child is much more likely than not to be able to handle some bad news; for instance, news in the form of "NO" without having to resort to justifying yourself or fearing a reaction to disappointment.
- **The inability to handle disappointment has been something that has characterized this child for some time.**

You have worked hard, and you now live in a different household than when you started P.A.C.T. You are predictable, consistent, and calm. Spike is civil to you. He seems like he cares. P.A.C.T. will stick with you forever; you will drop the goals that aren't relevant and continue those that are. You will wonder why everyone else with a child like Spike doesn't do the same. The payoff for learning your distance is a child who will develop into a functioning adult, occasionally flawed, but seeking solutions to things you can't supply.

There can be no hint of arbitrariness or equivocation in this goal. While your child is better able to hear disappointment, he still can't handle ambiguity. Thus, instructions and expectations need to be clear and stated in as few words as possible.

- **As a function of struggling through P.A.C.T., you have carved yourself into a piece of granite.** Granite is very predictable. It does not change. Granite today is the same as granite tomorrow.
- **It is very satisfying to Spike to notice that you are the same every day and to be able to count on your predictable strength.** He used to think that you were consistently weak, so weak that he could manipulate you into anger. You can't surprise granite.
- **We are all the best teachers of ourselves, so this should not be a problem.** However, your ability to reward works much better now, as it does not automatically result in an entitlement grab. All Spike ever wanted was for his parents to be parents, perhaps something of mythical parents, but parents nonetheless.

## What's the Last Word?

Living with a tough child is tough, but every day try to do the following in some combination: Look your child in the eye, smile often, give a gentle touch, and say something pleasant. And unloving, though they may be, see if you can tell them once a week that you do, in fact, love them. If you can't, don't worry about it. Some day you may be able to. You have plenty of time.

# CHAPTER 9 : Finale

## So Now What?

- **You have dragged yourself through this program and have some decent results.** You have learned that detaching yourself from provocation isn't impossible and that it feels good. You've learned that your child became dependent on your anger and everything that went with it a long time ago but that he was willing to give up his dependency when you did. Yes, you were dependent upon his anger, too. Your life was a continual tennis match.
- **You've learned that family life in general is much more peaceful.** You learned that you can all be together and actually like the experience. You've learned that your child has a future. You've also learned that your child needs to do things in his own way and in his own time but that he will probably do them if left to his own devices.
- **What's the future like?** Well, it is likely that all the work you have done will pay dividends for a long time. But it is also true that your child, however well he may have responded to your efforts, is still and will remain more sensitive than most, more easily threatened than most, more defensive than most and less self confident than most. This means that you will continue to use the program, which, for the most part, won't be a problem. You have permanently changed how you interact and react because you have become aware of pressure points that you did not know existed. You are now tuned in to your child in a way that you never were before. Your child will probably stumble here and there on his way to success. He may bring exquisite pain to you yet. The acute misery that you experienced with this child may come roaring back at you on occasion. You may wonder if all the effort you went through mattered at all. But it did.

> Spike needs time to understand what his old sense of rejection means. He has emotional mud dried on his boots that needs to come off. The mud influences everything. It will take him time to accept that parents are human. First, he must accept himself. All parents can do is what you've done: create a vehicle for acceptance to happen.

The upset will be less painful than it would if you had not struggled with this program. He is likely to get over his misery sooner, and you can have the assurance that you did not contribute to it. How do you know that any of this is true? Because, in spite of bumps in the road, you will have an overall sense of justified optimism about this child that transcends the bumps. You did not have this kind of optimism before.

- **You will, from time to time, wish that you could have a more spontaneous relationship with him rather than one that is measured and careful.** It is a natural longing. It is likely to be a while before this happens. It will seem wonderful when it does.

- **Developing self confidence after it has been thoroughly trashed takes time and may never rise to the level that it might have had if your child had not experienced so much unhappiness.** But your child's talents will shine through in time and both you and he can expect him to lead a decent life.

- **Even though this may seem an underwhelming conclusion, you will also likely become an acolyte of P.A.C.T., urging all whom you think could profit to enroll.** You will likely volunteer to be a mentor to new clients, offer endorsements to anyone who will listen and otherwise swear that you will get P.A.C.T. on every talk show in the nation. All of this is commonplace. Learning P.A.C.T. is like losing 100 pounds. You are likely to be exhilarated. Unlike weight loss, once you learn P.A.C.T., it is yours for life. It's like learning to ride a bike. P.A.C.T. will be your pal forever.

> You have given Spike a new life. You've removed pressure. His meanness and disrespect have dissipated. His education, his friends and his sense of responsibility look good or at least, better. He is more apt to accept authority. He is governed by his own clock. You can't push him any faster than he will go. He will slip, but he will pick himself up. His judgement won't always be best, but it will be good more often than bad. He may be isolated, fearful of new things, not very trusting or touchy, but he will also be loving. Life looks good. Congratulations. Take yourself out to dinner.

- **Clients who are just completing this training often want to know what the next step should be for them.** They say that they need some more. This probably is not true. They need the self-confidence that comes from saying goodbye to the trainer (if they used one) or the book and doing this program by themselves. The next step is real life.

# Appendix

**What a Great Idea!**

Go visit your parents. That's right. Spike's Mom did and thinks you should, too. Why? Well, Spike doesn't like his parents much, right? Things are much better, true, but he still holds them responsible for a lot that happened. Time is required for forgiveness. Well, his parents don't like their parents much either. Nothing unusual about this situation. Dysfunction, after all, tends to be multigenerational. Everybody gripes about their childhood, generally with reason. Given the increased attention paid to childrens' rights, there is a general feeling that our childhoods are supposed to be perfect. It isn't going to happen, Not with most of us. It really puts most parents in an impossible position.

So, we gripe. Spike's Mom just happened to spend the weekend with her folks at about the end of this program. She left the children, the dog and the husband at home. She was astonished. She saw for the first time where the things that she had been battling in P.A.C.T. came from. She saw anger, pointless arguments, passive aggressiveness, and a bunch of other stuff in her parents that she never saw before. She wondered how she could have missed it. Everything just leaped out at her. She saw how she must have been trained as a child to cope with difficulty. She saw that she was trained to be angry. Her parents tried to solve problems with anger, argument, conflict, etc. The training was effective, but the visit wasn't good. She evidently learned a lot, and a lot came back to bite her.

She had always been led to believe that she was "wrong." She felt blamed. In fact, her folks have been no help whatsoever when it came to Spike. They didn't visit. They didn't sympathize. They said Spike and all the chaos around him was her fault. They said she was too lenient. They said she needed to show Spike who was boss. They understood nothing.

She now understands that her deficiencies were nurtured. Does it change a lot? Probably not. But it is comforting, in a sense, to see that if she was nuts, then by God, everyone around her was nuts, too.

This is not a time to settle scores. You will learn, if you don't know already, that you can't change your parents. You will have to come to terms with the fact that they are the way they are. Spike doesn't know it, but he faces the exact same thing except in his case, his parents struggled to make big changes in how they interacted with him. They are likely to be more open than his grandparents. So there will be an openness that was not present in his mom's relationship with her parents. But just on the off chance that maybe one of her parents could hear her, Spike's Mom approached her father as you may approach your father: "So, Dad, I don't think I ever knew how much you and Mom fought. Was it always like this?" "Nevermind about that. I don't know what you're talking about. Forget it." "I can't. I think it set me up for my troubles with Spike. When I used to look in the mirror, I would see you or Mom. I didn't always like what I saw. I didn't understand it until now."

The conversation, of course, didn't end well. You need to be prepared for the same. P.A.C.T. is a struggle. Sometimes it seems as if you take two steps forward and one back and all you can remember is the backward step. It is comforting to visit where much of it was developed and realize that you have, indeed, made lots of progress. Happy visit.

### Remember Angelique?

Angelique has been seen, but she hasn't been heard, not since Part I, anyway. This is not a surprise. Many P.A.C.T. families have more than one child. One will be terrible. The other will be wonderful. The "other" isn't a central character. She plays the walk-on in someone else's drama. Still, it is good to have one of both. If one makes you feel like a failure, you can take comfort in the other.

Sort of. The other is a time bomb. The explosion can happen one of two ways. First, the other may get tired of being wonderful. As the atmosphere of the household changes, the nice one will grab some of the attention. She will be as foul as the bad one. Parents will assume the program has failed. It hasn't. Parents need to continue with the good child the way they did with the bad child. The rebellion will simmer down. The good child really isn't into being an oppositional rebel. She is into: "See me! See me! I'm over here!" she says, jumping up and down at the far end of the family football field. She would like to shed her transparency. The rebel stuff will be temporary if parents are cool. But if Angelique doesn't display her 15 minutes of rebellion on your football field, she gives us a second option.

Option Two: Angelique skips the rebellion. Everything is fine: school, friends and chores. She sings in the church choir, has a paper route and feeds the dog. What a marvelous child. She also continues in her role as the forgotten child, competent and largely quiet. Her willingness to do well is an example of her independence. She can't rely on family. Family has not been there for her in the past. It isn't there for her now. They assume she can take care of herself. The bad child sucked the oxygen out of the household. He was the focus of everything. And, to some extent, still is. She was an orphan before. She is an orphan still. But it isn't a problem. Yet.

A needed digression: There are fewer things more galling than to be raised by a reformed alcoholic. Alcoholic families go through hell. But sometimes those parents pull themselves together, triumph over their alcoholism, go to meetings and are, in effect, reborn. What does the family think about all this? They are glad the booze is gone. But they may get a born-again, sober, paragon of virtue to deal with in exchange. Maybe it is the mom. If so, mom constantly misses dinner with her family. She is out giving presentations on the dangers of raising children in an alcoholic home to any group who will have her. All the damage that this mom created did not magically go away just because she gave up the bottle. The resentment continues. The sense of abandonment hasn't stopped. Instead of booze, now they must live with a parent who is absorbed in virtue. Life has always been about the boozer. Now it's about the boozer's sobriety. So, in a sense, it is still all about the booze. It is too much. There is work to be done with the children who get left behind.

Back to Option Two: Angelique is the left-behind child in our story. What did she get out of all the change? The household is easier. She isn't antagonized by Spike anymore. She can bring her friends over. This is all good. Spike complained about his parents never being there for him. Well, guess what? Angelique does, too. Angelique gets stuck at home with fast food for dinner because her parents go to P.A.C.T. presentations and tell other families how much their lives have been changed. Fast forward to Angelique's adulthood:

Angelique, graduated from college (she beat Spike), dumped her old boyfriend. Her parents worried about her choice. The old boyfriend was eerily like the old Spike: angry, isolated, chip on the shoulder, fearful, aggressive, and hyper-sensitive. Funny, how we gravitate to things we know. Life was all about the boyfriend's unhappiness. She found someone new: upbeat, disciplined, eager, friendly, confident. They marry. Careers are assembled. The babies arrive. Angelique's sense of how to be a mother is partially motivated by what a lousy job she thinks you did as a parent. By contrast, she is one terrific parent. You are delighted, of course, but pained as well. She turns her sense of orphan into pushing you away. You weren't there for her earlier. Now she isn't there for you. She can't decide what she wants from you: Go away! Get involved! Both! You step off on the left foot, she wants the right. Expectations are high. When you slip, she reminds you. Brother, is this ever familiar.

Bummer.

You made the mistake of assuming that since Spike was hard, you could get a margin of sympathy out of Angelique. Think again, Bozo. (Sorry, but if you aren't tipped off, you will feel like a clown). You don't get to relax just yet. There is now a bond between Angelique and Spike; that bond is their recollection of your incompetence. They have little else in common.

Damn.

Don't despair. Part of this rings a bit hollow…afterall Angelique is a successful human being. Good marriage, career, family, and attitude. She won't fall apart. She won't hit bottom. She won't go anywhere but up. You have not failed. Remember: If you have the responsibility for one of those children wrapped around your neck, you get the other one, too. It is also perfectly true that her success happened BECAUSE she was the forgotten child. If she got the same parenting that Spike thought he got, she'd be a mess, too. As if she really wanted to share the same canoe with her brother! You can forgive her if she is not quite clear on these matters.

But you are disappointed that you don't have the relationship you hoped you'd have. At least not yet. You have time to create it. You just won't get the mug next week that says, "World's Greatest Mom." Hurt? Sure it hurts.

But her feelings are her feelings. They matter. You can negotiate those rocks. You did with Spike and that was vastly more work. This takes mostly patience. Turns out Spike isn't the only person who must learn how to forgive. All things considered, it is better to have an Option One Angelique. But you may not be so lucky. Therapy, anyone?

# Quiz #1: The Thumbnail Scale

How much are you like other successful P.A.C.T. clients?

1. Does your family live in continual and mutual conflict?
2. Is your child nearly or completely out of your control?
3. Does your child have a psychiatric label or the behaviors that would get him/her one?
4. Have you participated in virtually all services available to you?
5. Do you like this child well enough to make a big sacrifice for him/her?
6. Are you opposed to any out-of-home placement for this child? Are you worried about reunification?
7. Are you at risk for losing your child to an ex-spouse or State Child Protection due to his behavior?
8. Are your mental health needs sufficiently mild or sufficiently under control that you can enroll in a program that makes significant self-discipline demands?
9. Are you desperate?
10. Are you willing to undertake a program that makes you the focus of change, rather than your child?
11. Is P.A.C.T. something that you want to learn?

Prospective clients normally check off at least 9.

Caveat: The presence of depression or anxiety may have an impact on how efficiently the program is learned. Often the only way to know for certain is to begin the program. Most clients notice small but convincing change in about 8 weeks if the program has been followed carefully. All timing varies from client to client as well as outcomes for parents and children.

# Quiz #2: The Parent Self-Rating Scale

This quiz reveals who takes ownership of the problems in your household. Select only one of the following answers for each of the 10 questions.

1. Which family member hits?
2. Which family member swears?
3. Which family member gets angry easily?
4. Which family member is most critical?
5. Which family is mean?
6. Which family member is rude?
7. Which family member calls names?
8. Which family member is difficult?
9. Which family member argues?
10. Which family member yells?

Scoring: Give yourself 1 point for each "both parent and child"; 2 points for each "just the parent"; 3 points for each "just the child"; 4 points for each "neither parent nor child". The score range 1 to 40. The most successful clients have the smallest numbers.

| | YELL | ANGER | DISTRACT | SURPRISE | THREATEN | SWEAR | TONE | SARCASM | CRITICISM | NAG | FOLLOW | PREACH | DEALS | BUTTONS | DEMAND | ACCUSE | ARGUE | COMPLAIN | NAMES | REASON | QUESTION | FRUSTRATE | CONVERSATION | DREDGE | EXPLAIN | NEGATIVE | PASSIVE-AGGRESSIVE | WAFFLE | TOTALS |
|---|---|---|---|---|---|---|---|---|---|---|---|---|---|---|---|---|---|---|---|---|---|---|---|---|---|---|---|---|---|
| WEEK 1 | | | | | | | | | | | | | | | | | | | | | | | | | | | | | |
| WEEK 2 | | | | | | | | | | | | | | | | | | | | | | | | | | | | | |
| WEEK 3 | | | | | | | | | | | | | | | | | | | | | | | | | | | | | |
| WEEK 4 | | | | | | | | | | | | | | | | | | | | | | | | | | | | | |
| WEEK 5 | | | | | | | | | | | | | | | | | | | | | | | | | | | | | |
| WEEK 6 | | | | | | | | | | | | | | | | | | | | | | | | | | | | | |
| WEEK 7 | | | | | | | | | | | | | | | | | | | | | | | | | | | | | |
| WEEK 8 | | | | | | | | | | | | | | | | | | | | | | | | | | | | | |
| WEEK 9 | | | | | | | | | | | | | | | | | | | | | | | | | | | | | |
| WEEK 10 | | | | | | | | | | | | | | | | | | | | | | | | | | | | | |
| WEEK 11 | | | | | | | | | | | | | | | | | | | | | | | | | | | | | |
| WEEK 12 | | | | | | | | | | | | | | | | | | | | | | | | | | | | | |
| WEEK 13 | | | | | | | | | | | | | | | | | | | | | | | | | | | | | |

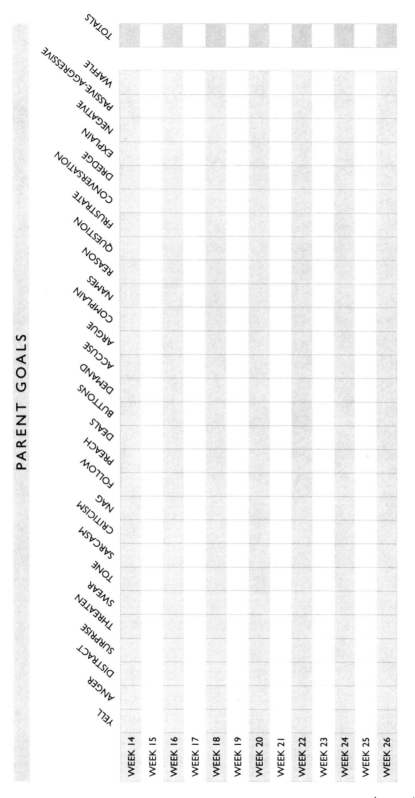

PARENT GOALS

TOTALS

WAFFLE
PASSIVE-AGGRESSIVE
NEGATIVE
EXPLAIN
DREDGE
CONVERSATION
FRUSTRATE
QUESTION
REASON
NAMES
COMPLAIN
ARGUE
ACCUSE
DEMAND
BUTTONS
DEALS
PREACH
FOLLOW
NAG
CRITICISM
SARCASM
TONE
SWEAR
THREATEN
SURPRISE
DISTRACT
ANGER
YELL

WEEK 14
WEEK 15
WEEK 16
WEEK 17
WEEK 18
WEEK 19
WEEK 20
WEEK 21
WEEK 22
WEEK 23
WEEK 24
WEEK 25
WEEK 26

Appendix     157

## PARENT GOALS

| | YELL | ANGER | DISTRACT | SURPRISE | THREATEN | SWEAR | TONE | SARCASM | CRITICISM | NAG | FOLLOW | PREACH | DEALS | BUTTONS | DEMAND | ACCUSE | ARGUE | COMPLAIN | NAMES | REASON | QUESTION | FRUSTRATE | CONVERSATION | DREDGE | EXPLAIN | NEGATIVE | PASSIVE-AGGRESSIVE | WAFFLE | TOTALS |
|---|---|---|---|---|---|---|---|---|---|---|---|---|---|---|---|---|---|---|---|---|---|---|---|---|---|---|---|---|---|
| WEEK 27 | | | | | | | | | | | | | | | | | | | | | | | | | | | | | |
| WEEK 28 | | | | | | | | | | | | | | | | | | | | | | | | | | | | | |
| WEEK 29 | | | | | | | | | | | | | | | | | | | | | | | | | | | | | |
| WEEK 30 | | | | | | | | | | | | | | | | | | | | | | | | | | | | | |
| WEEK 31 | | | | | | | | | | | | | | | | | | | | | | | | | | | | | |
| WEEK 32 | | | | | | | | | | | | | | | | | | | | | | | | | | | | | |
| WEEK 33 | | | | | | | | | | | | | | | | | | | | | | | | | | | | | |
| WEEK 34 | | | | | | | | | | | | | | | | | | | | | | | | | | | | | |
| WEEK 35 | | | | | | | | | | | | | | | | | | | | | | | | | | | | | |
| WEEK 36 | | | | | | | | | | | | | | | | | | | | | | | | | | | | | |
| WEEK 37 | | | | | | | | | | | | | | | | | | | | | | | | | | | | | |
| WEEK 38 | | | | | | | | | | | | | | | | | | | | | | | | | | | | | |
| WEEK 39 | | | | | | | | | | | | | | | | | | | | | | | | | | | | | |

| | YELL | ANGER | DISTRACT | SURPRISE | THREATEN | SWEAR | TONE | SARCASM | CRITICISM | NAG | FOLLOW | PREACH | DEALS | BUTTONS | DEMAND | ACCUSE | ARGUE | COMPLAIN | NAMES | REASON | QUESTION | FRUSTRATE | CONVERSATION | DREDGE | EXPLAIN | NEGATIVE | PASSIVE-AGGRESSIVE | WAFFLE | TOTALS |
|---|---|---|---|---|---|---|---|---|---|---|---|---|---|---|---|---|---|---|---|---|---|---|---|---|---|---|---|---|---|
| WEEK 40 | | | | | | | | | | | | | | | | | | | | | | | | | | | | | |
| WEEK 41 | | | | | | | | | | | | | | | | | | | | | | | | | | | | | |
| WEEK 42 | | | | | | | | | | | | | | | | | | | | | | | | | | | | | |
| WEEK 43 | | | | | | | | | | | | | | | | | | | | | | | | | | | | | |
| WEEK 44 | | | | | | | | | | | | | | | | | | | | | | | | | | | | | |
| WEEK 45 | | | | | | | | | | | | | | | | | | | | | | | | | | | | | |
| WEEK 46 | | | | | | | | | | | | | | | | | | | | | | | | | | | | | |
| WEEK 47 | | | | | | | | | | | | | | | | | | | | | | | | | | | | | |
| WEEK 48 | | | | | | | | | | | | | | | | | | | | | | | | | | | | | |
| WEEK 49 | | | | | | | | | | | | | | | | | | | | | | | | | | | | | |
| WEEK 50 | | | | | | | | | | | | | | | | | | | | | | | | | | | | | |
| WEEK 51 | | | | | | | | | | | | | | | | | | | | | | | | | | | | | |
| WEEK 52 | | | | | | | | | | | | | | | | | | | | | | | | | | | | | |

# CHILD GOALS

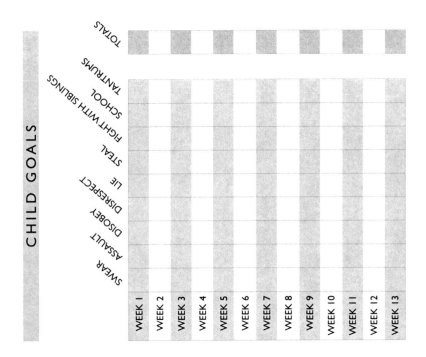

| | SWEAR | ASSAULT | DISOBEY | DISRESPECT | LIE | STEAL | FIGHT WITH SIBLINGS | SCHOOL | TANTRUMS | TOTALS |
|---|---|---|---|---|---|---|---|---|---|---|
| WEEK 1 | | | | | | | | | | |
| WEEK 2 | | | | | | | | | | |
| WEEK 3 | | | | | | | | | | |
| WEEK 4 | | | | | | | | | | |
| WEEK 5 | | | | | | | | | | |
| WEEK 6 | | | | | | | | | | |
| WEEK 7 | | | | | | | | | | |
| WEEK 8 | | | | | | | | | | |
| WEEK 9 | | | | | | | | | | |
| WEEK 10 | | | | | | | | | | |
| WEEK 11 | | | | | | | | | | |
| WEEK 12 | | | | | | | | | | |
| WEEK 13 | | | | | | | | | | |

# CHILD GOALS

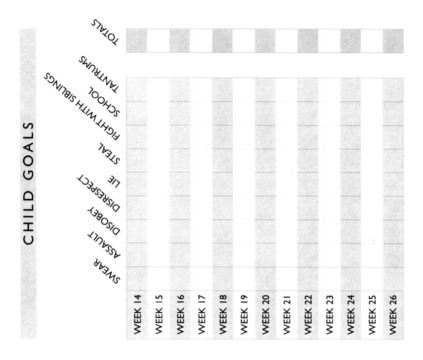

| | SWEAR | ASSAULT | DISOBEY | DISRESPECT | LIE | STEAL | FIGHT WITH SIBLINGS | SCHOOL | TANTRUMS | TOTALS |
|---|---|---|---|---|---|---|---|---|---|---|
| WEEK 14 | | | | | | | | | | |
| WEEK 15 | | | | | | | | | | |
| WEEK 16 | | | | | | | | | | |
| WEEK 17 | | | | | | | | | | |
| WEEK 18 | | | | | | | | | | |
| WEEK 19 | | | | | | | | | | |
| WEEK 20 | | | | | | | | | | |
| WEEK 21 | | | | | | | | | | |
| WEEK 22 | | | | | | | | | | |
| WEEK 23 | | | | | | | | | | |
| WEEK 24 | | | | | | | | | | |
| WEEK 25 | | | | | | | | | | |
| WEEK 26 | | | | | | | | | | |

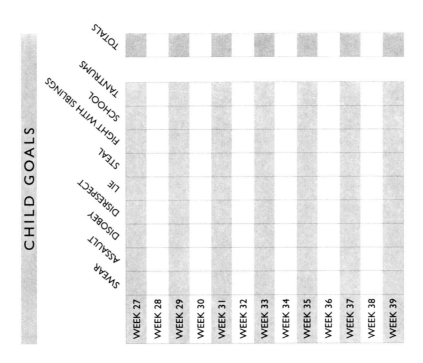

# CHILD GOALS

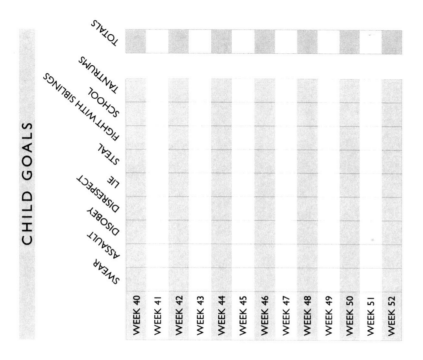

|  | SWEAR | ASSAULT | DISOBEY | DISRESPECT | LIE | STEAL | FIGHT WITH SIBLINGS | SCHOOL | TANTRUMS | TOTALS |
|---|---|---|---|---|---|---|---|---|---|---|
| WEEK 40 |  |  |  |  |  |  |  |  |  |  |
| WEEK 41 |  |  |  |  |  |  |  |  |  |  |
| WEEK 42 |  |  |  |  |  |  |  |  |  |  |
| WEEK 43 |  |  |  |  |  |  |  |  |  |  |
| WEEK 44 |  |  |  |  |  |  |  |  |  |  |
| WEEK 45 |  |  |  |  |  |  |  |  |  |  |
| WEEK 46 |  |  |  |  |  |  |  |  |  |  |
| WEEK 47 |  |  |  |  |  |  |  |  |  |  |
| WEEK 48 |  |  |  |  |  |  |  |  |  |  |
| WEEK 49 |  |  |  |  |  |  |  |  |  |  |
| WEEK 50 |  |  |  |  |  |  |  |  |  |  |
| WEEK 51 |  |  |  |  |  |  |  |  |  |  |
| WEEK 52 |  |  |  |  |  |  |  |  |  |  |

Robert Ingersoll said that, "In nature there are no rewards or punishments, just consequences."

P.A.C.T. says, there are in fact all kinds of consequences for Spike's behavior; they just happen not to be within parental control and don't feel like consequences to parents anyway, since they don't involve torture.

# Bibliography

Arnold, J. C. (2006) *Why forgive.* New York: Orbis.

Barkley, R. A. (1997) *ADHD and the nature of self-control.* New York: The Guilford Press.

Bowlby, J. (1988) *A secure base: parent-child attachment and healthy human development.* New York: Basic Books.

Bradshaw, J. (1996) *Bradshaw on: the family.* Deerfield Beach: Health Communications.

Gauld, L. and Gauld, M. (2002) *The biggest job we'll ever have.* New York: Scribner.

Greene, R. W. (2001) *The explosive child.* New York: Quill.

Greven, P. (1992) *Spare the child: the religious roots of punishment and the psychological impact of physical abuse.* New York: Vintage.

Hulbert, A. (2003) *Raising america: experts, parents and a century of advice about children.* New York: Alfred A. Knopf.

Kazdin, A. E. (1994) *Behavior modification.* Pacific Grove: Brooks Cole.

Lamb, S. (1996) *The trouble with blame.* Cambridge: Harvard University Press.

LaRossa, R. (1997) *The modernization of fatherhood.* Chicago: The University of Chicago Press.

Leedom, L. J. (2006) *Just like his father.* Fairfield: Healing Arts.

O'Donnell, J.M. (1985) *The origins of behaviorism: american psychology,* 1870-1920. New York: New York University Press.

Rekowski, L. (2006) *A victim no more.* Charlottesville: Hampton Roads.

Smedes, L. B. (1996) *The art of forgiving*. New York: Ballantine Books.

Stearns, C. Z. and Stearns, P. N. (1986) *Anger: the struggle for emotional control in america's history*. Chicago: The University of Chicago Press.

Stearns, P. N. (1989) *Jealousy: the evolution of an emotion in american history*. New York: New York University Press.

Sternberg, R. J. and Barnes, M. L. (1988) *The psychology of love*. New Haven: Yale University Press.

Van Hasselt, V. B. and Hersen, M. (1995) *Handbook of adolescent psychopathology: a guide to diagnosis and treatment*. New York: The Free Press.

# About the Author

Peter Polomski, The Lily Pad

Dr. Andrew Gibson was born in 1945. He grew up in the Midwest and graduated from Ironwood High School in the upper peninsula of Michigan. There he developed a fondness for pasties (Cornish meat pies) and makes the best ones ever. It is the crust that distinguishes his from others with its heavenly combination of lard and suet. He spends a great deal of time in the gym as a result. He joined the Navy and was assigned to a Fleet Marine Force during the Vietnam war. He got his undergraduate and master's degree from San Diego State University and taught at Portland State University in Oregon and the University of Maine in Presque Isle. He received his Ph. D. From the University of Connecticut where he studied with the fabled Dr. Richard Bloomer. He developed P.A.C.T. Training while he was a School Psychologist and ultimately devoted himself to its full time practice. He lives in a quintessential New England village in Connecticut with his wife of 41 years. They have no pets with cute names. They do have two sons who are busy raising their own families and pulling careers together. For more information about Dr. Gibson and the Parenting Angry Children and Teens (P.A.C.T.) Program, please visit www.DrAGibson.com

# INDEX

CPSIA information can be obtained at www.ICGtesting.com

264970BV00004B/1-2/P